The Secret Life Of Walter Winchell

LYLE STUART

BARRICADE
BOOKS

FORT LEE, NEW JERSEY

Published by Barricade Books Inc.
185 Bridge Plaza North
Suite 308-A
Fort Lee, NJ 07024
www.barricadebooks.com

Library of Congress Cataloging-in-Publication Data

Stuart, Lyle.
    The secret life of Walter Winchell / Lyle Stuart.
        p. cm.
    ISBN 1-56980-251-3 (pbk.)
    1. Winchell, Walter, 1897-1972. 2. Gossip columnists--United States--
Biography. I. Title.

PN4874.W67S7 2003
070.92--dc21
[B]
                                                                2003040418
First Printing Barricade Books Edition
Manufactured in Canada

to all those
who have ever been hurt
by irresponsible gossip-columnists

If the divines do rightly infer from the sixth commandment, *Thou shalt not kill*—scandalizing one's neighbor with false and malicious reports, whereby I vex his spirit, and consequently impair his health, is a degree of murder.

Sir Walter Raleigh

PROEM

The book you hold in your hands made quite a bit of history. The author, yours truly, was attacked by three hired thugs for writing it. He identified two of them from a police mug book and they were arrested, tried and convicted. They received one year prison sentences.

A primary source of information for this book was Winchell's former son-in-law. He was sent to prison for five years on a trumped-up income tax evasion charge.

This book's original publisher, Samuel Roth, also went to prison for five years on charges that had little to do with why the Justice Department came after him. It was, as Freedom of Information documents revealed, solely because he dared to publish this book. His conviction resulted in the U.S. Supreme Court's Roth obscenity decision.

After the two men went to the penitentiary, Winchell told me to my face that I would be next. I told him I was packed and ready.

In the years that followed, I sued Winchell three times for libel and collected every time. I used $8,000 of this money to start a book publishing company which grew to where it was sold in 1989 for $12.5 million. Incidentally, my third lawsuit was used by the American Broadcasting Company as a ruse to end Winchell's television career.

Walter Winchell was, in his time, the most powerful journalist in the world. He described gossip as "...the art of saying nothing in a way that leaves practically nothing unsaid."

Winchell could put people in jail with the help of his close friend, the closet queen J. Edgar Hoover who ran the F.B.I. as a personal preserve. You can find all 3,908 pages of the 30-year correspondence between Winchell and Hoover on the internet.

Walter Winchell could, all by himself, make a corporation's

stock rise or fall with a single sentence spoken on his Sunday night radio broadcast. He could rescue a badly panned Broadway show open after it received unanimous bad reviews and turn it into a smash hit with his constant column plugs. Example? *Hellzapoppin'*.

Similarly, he could make or break a new film with a single mention in his column or on his broadcast.

The Winchell column appeared in more than 2,000 newspapers around the world. His broadcast (and later, telecast) could be heard even by those who didn't own a radio if they walked down any residential street at 9 PM on Sunday night. Everybody's radio was tuned in to Winchell.

But things change and circumstance took a hand. The parade passed him by.

When he died in 1972, he was a broken man, forgotten, ignored, powerless. At his burial in Greenwood Memorial Lawn in Phoenix, Arizona, the only mourner at his graveside was Walda, one of his three children.

Nevertheless, on his death, *The New York Times* eulogized him in a page one obituary that described him as "the country's best-known and most widely known journalist as well as among its most influential."

The Secret Life of Walter Winchell affected many lives, not the least of which was his. When originally published, many bookshops were afraid to stock it. On the other hand, Winchell was feuding with the Copacabana nightclub because they'd fired a chorus girl with whom he was having an affair. He attacked the club regularly until he learned that it was buying 50 copies a day of this book to distribute as gifts to its patrons.

All attacks ceased immediately.

Long out-of-print and bringing a high price in the rare book market, *The Secret Life of Walter Winchell* has been published again because Barricade Books felt it was time to make this title one of its Cult Classics.

— Lyle Stuart
Stuyvesant, NY
June 2003

Epilogue in Advance

A few days after this book was completed, a strange thing happened to its author.

On the morning of August 11, 1953, the author, upon leaving his home in North Bergen, New Jersey, at 8:35 A.M. was set upon by three men, who attempted to beat him into unconsciousness with a blackjack and with their fists.

The beating was similar to two beatings given a New York radio commentator who had been consistently critical of Walter Winchell.

It had this variation.

The author fought off his attackers, secured the license number of their getaway car, and was able to make positive identification of two of the three men from rogues' gallery photographs. The auto license number belonged to one of the identified men.

The two men were waterfront thugs. Both had long records of arrests and convictions for such crimes as brutal and atrocious assault with intent to kill.

At the time of the attack on the author, both men were out on bail ($40,000 each) in connection with a bomb-throwing incident.

The two men have been arrested. They have not yet revealed who, if anyone, put them up to the attack.

The reader like the author—who was given no clue to the origin or purpose of the attack—is left to seek an explanation.

7

1. A Name to Reckon With

His typewriter is still tapping. The fedora of the most widely-read gossiper in history sits on his balding head as he faces microphone and television camera for his Sunday night simulcast.

Walter Winchell.

The name is already part of the legend of the past.

Walter Winchell.

The go-getter man who got to be King of the hill. The fast-talking know-it-all who looked down upon his America barking praise, burping disapproval.

He began by talking to himself, and within a decade had become the most widely read columnist and most listened to commentator in the history of the world. More people read him daily than have read Shakespeare through the centuries.

In his thin fingers he held the absolute power of the press. His was the power to make or break a theatrical show, an artist, a book, a political career. It was all his. He played with it. He toyed with it.

He taught Americans never to underestimate the power of the printed gossip, of the widespread word.

Who and what is the real Winchell? How has he been able to keep his private affairs private while making the private affairs of other men public?

His private life he has wanted to keep very private.

There were things about his own life that would not

look good in print. And there have not been men who would dare his wrath by printing them.

Walter Winchell.

A name to reckon with.

He has money, power and fame.

Yet none of these can cover his nakedness, the itching goading quagmire of insecurity in which he flounders. It drove him to the top, and is responsible for what is happening to him now.

He can remember the gone days when he was the center of a hubbub of acclaim. But he cannot retrace his steps.

The myths that he planted about himself have blossomed and died. The bouquets he threw at himself have faded and shrunk.

"I'm Winchell," he shouted recently. "Don't you understand? I'm Winchell!"

The earth, if it heard, paid no immediate attention but continued to turn gently on its axis.

2

Beginner's Luck

In the year 1874, Alexander Winchell wrote his "Sketches of Creation" which was published by Harper and Brothers.

Seven years later he spoke before the Summer School of Christian Principle on "The Speculative Consequences of Evolution."

There is no indication that anything in either the lecture or the book anticipated Walter Winchell.

In 1910 when Walter Winchell was working as an usher after school at the Imperial Theater on the East Side of Manhattan, Alexander's brother, Horace Newton Winchell was putting the finishing touches to a study on the Aborigines of Minnesota.

Walter's formal education was finished one year later. He would never read "The Aborigines of Minnesota" and no doubt "The Speculative Consequences of Evolution" were beyond the ken of a man whose knowledge was so limited that he thought Emile Zola was a woman and that Paris was a seaport.

On the other hand, it is doubtful if either Alexander or Horace Newton Winchell ever heard of Walter, or would ever read a "Winchell" column.

Today the Encyclopedias Americana and Britannica both give brief biographies of Alexander and Horace Winchell.

There is no mention of Walter Winchell.

He has tried to scratch his mark on the face of the

earth, but he has scratched in sand and sand does not hold its form.

The genealogy on the name Winchell says in part:

"There is little doubt that the family name of the Winchells is derived from the name of a place, and it seems most probable that it comes from the name of a town called Winchelsea, which was once an important port in England.

"Family names did not exist commonly in England earlier than the fourteenth century. Just before and during the time when such names were gradually adopted, old records show that persons were commonly known by such names as 'William de Winchelcumbe,' 'Stephen de Wynshull,' and 'Walter de Wincalton.'

"The preposition 'de' means of, and these names mean respectively: William of (the town or monastery of) Winchelcumbe; Stephen of (the town of) Wynshull; and Walter of (the town of) Wyncalton (known also as Winchaulton about 1240 and now called Wincanton)."

The Winchell name has been traced back to 1412. Winchell ancestors were of Welsh nativity and it is not at all unlikely that Saxons bearing the name migrated to Wales in the 15th or 16th century.

When Walter Winchell's ancestors migrated to America from eastern Europe, they may have selected the name Winschel without any knowledge of the Winchells already in this country.

There was a George W. Winchell who was an editor. He was also a member of the G.A.R., the Masons and the Odd Fellows. He died in 1897, the year Walter was born.

Oddly enough, Joseph Rice Winchell also died in 1897. He too was an editor and made many enemies in Missouri because of his staunch patriotism at the time of the Civil War.

His life was often in danger. At one time guerrillas surrounded his house and searched it with the intention of killing him. He eluded them by hiding among some clothes in a small hall room.

Walter Winchell fits into none of this.

His father, Jacob Laino alias Jake Lipsky alias Jacob Winschel was a sex pervert who molested small girls.

One of Winchell's earliest memories (he was six at the time) was the nightmarish scene of his father running down the street toward him with a crowd in chase who were stoning him and tossing filth from the gutter onto him. He had attempted to lure a ten year old child into a tenement basement.

Jacob Laino, as he was known to the police, was arrested twice. The effect of the scandal on the two Winchell children was indicative of things to come. Al meekly swallowed the taunts and obscenities of the street gangs. In school, when a teacher referred to his father, he broke down and cried. Today Al is an unassuming unheralded little-known accountant who rides the BMT and is concerned with the rising subway fares.

Walter swore back at the street gangs. He would shout obscenities in their faces and then run. He could outtalk them and he was a faster runner than his hecklers. He talked and then he ran fast.

He has been running ever since.

The Winschel household was a railroad flat, a long hallway with two appendages that were small rooms. In the summer they would be heat-baked, in the winter they would be chilled boxes.

There was a public toilet in the house. It needed a coat of paint. On its walls were epigrams and a verse or two written by the "columnists" of the house.

There was a line written on the hallway with pencil. It was a poor parody of Jack the Ripper.

Jake the Raper, it said, referring to the elder Winschel.

Mrs. Winschel futilely tried to scrub the line from the wall.

Winchell found her fighting the paint, weeping softly to herself.

The ten year old boy was hard as nails. "Mama, let's get away from him. He's no good. He's a rat."

There was a sharp slap, and Winchell spun, stunned. "Why do you hit me?" he screamed. "I didn't do nothing!"

There were creaking sounds as neighbors began to open their doors just slightly, just enough to hear.

"Quiet," muttered the mother. "You mustn't talk that way about your own father."

He didn't answer. He stumbled up the stairs.

"You'll turn out just like him. You'll be a no good bum, saying things about your own father."

But in the apartment there had been a perpetual battle between the parents. Sometimes Jacob Winschel didn't come home, and the mother would send Al to fetch him. He could usually be found standing on the street, bargaining with the local prostitutes.

Sometimes both father and mother would disappear for weeks, and the two Winschel boys would be boarded and fed by relatives. Eventually the relatives gave up and the boys were left with strangers.

The strangers received a few dollars a week for the use of one bed and three meals. Beyond that they assumed no responsibility. The two boys were allowed to shift for themselves.

When Walter played hooky from school and the truant officers complained to his temporary guardians, they simply shrugged their shoulders in unconcern.

The father and mother would come together, and the boys would be taken back into a makeshift apartment. This was the unhappiest time for the boys.

At night Walter would lie awake listening to the creaking of his parents' bed, listening to their muttering, their cursing of each other.

The elder Winschel would rarely bring home enough of his money to feed and clothe his family, even according to East Side tenement standards.

In his teens, Walter Winchell sometimes tried to weave

an imaginary Cinderella background for himself. His father, he said, was "a rich and successful silk merchant."

The "rich silk merchant" became the theme of an early publicity story about Winchell—and then it was dropped.

Silk merchants didn't live in East Side tenements with public toilets and bedbugs and the constant guttural voices of pushcart peddlers for street music. And too many of Winchell's playmates were still around who remembered the old man who accosted little girls.

When Winchell was twelve, Jacob Laino was carrying on a flirtation with a fourteen year old girl on the floor below. Her father threatened Jacob with a knife.

Winchell's mother sent him for the police. But when a patrolman arrived, Jacob's reputation was already such that the patrolman beat him with his club, while the mother and son stood helplessly by. When the father lay unconscious on the floor, Winchell's mother spat at the policeman and hurled epithets at him in Hebrew.

Eventually the parents parted. Mrs. Winschel wanted her husband to take one of the boys, but Jacob laughed at her.

They were divorced. It was the first divorce Walter Winchell ever knew about. It was the gossip of the neighborhood, where divorce was a rare thing among Jewish immigrants.

It was one of two divorces he would never write about in the column he would write when he grew up. (The other was his own.)

When the divorce became effective, the father disappeared. The two boys remained with their mother.

Although she seemed to care slightly for the younger boy, Al, Winchell's mother looked upon Walter as an intruder.

Winchell repaid her. Years later his mother would commit suicide after Walter Winchell forbade her to visit her grandchildren.

The soprano voice changed to a medium tenor.

The fatherless family, come upon hard times, moved to a one room and kitchen apartment. Walter and Al slept together on a cot in the kitchen.

Walter attended public school. At P.S. 184 he was registered Winchel rather than Winschel.

There was never a cent in the house to spare for pleasure. Walter would carefully hide his longing when his schoolmates drank ice-cream sodas at the neighborhood candy store. On Saturday morning the street gang would attend the local movie house. Walter, a hard-shelled personality already developing, announced that he had other things to do, "more important" things.

Weekday afternoons, there was punch ball. In the street. Sliding close to the horse manure. Racing to beat the catch. Amid the screams and shouts and snorts and smells that made the East Side a place to escape from.

Punch ball. It was played any place on the street. They played one sewer for home and the next sewer down the block for second; then halfway in between, on each side of the gutter, they laid out first and third.

Now they had a field and the only thing they had to do was punch the ball out and play like baseball.

Except for the pushcarts getting in the way, and the horse-drawn carriages and the dogs barking at their heels.

Walter Winchell was up. Two men on base. He hit a grounder between second and third. The ball was lost for a moment and then recovered.

Someone said, "That was some smack."

Winchell nodded. "It was easy. I could see the opening."

He kept on talking his head off. Telling anyone who would look or listen how he could see the opening and how he knew he would score.

"Don't get snotty about it," one of the players remarked. "You made the hit. So now forget it."

Winchell glowered.

He didn't take his eyes off the heckler. With the two in the field and the other team up, a ball came in the direction of the heckler. Winchell raced over, trying to catch the ball that was a natural catch for the heckler; trying to muscle in.

Blinded by his intensity, he didn't see the car coming, didn't hear its noisy engine. He was hit.

Police came. A horse-drawn ambulance arrived.

Walter Winchell was rushed to the hospital. "I'm dying!" he screamed. "That son of a bitch killed me!"

But at the hospital no serious injuries were found.

The next afternoon Winchell hopefully scanned the pages of the Evening Sun. The news was about President Taft. But a small two-paragraph item in the back of the paper told about the accident. Another boy hit by a wild driver. The driver had been speeding at thirty miles an hour.

Winchell proudly showed the clipping to the boys and girls in his class. They were impressed. The girls looked at him. He was keenly aware that for a day at least he was a kind of hero. He was credited with a narrow escape from death. His name in the newspaper did it.

Afternoons, after school, Walter Winchell got a part-time job as movie usher. He took tickets, sang along with slides, and sold candy.

A few weeks later at home in the kitchen he practiced a home-made song and dance act, while Al played a harmonica. It was a new song called "Will You Love Me In December As You Do In May?"

Winchell had learned the words from a ten cent song sheet at the theater. His sharp eyes noted the name of its writer. The writer was an aspiring songsmith and this was his first big hit. He would later become a friend of Winchell's and, more important, the Mayor of New York. The name on the song sheet was James J. Walker.

"What are you going to do?" Al asked between notes. He was impressed by Walter's ambition. He had little of his own.

"They need singing ushers at the 'Itch.' I figure I might make the grade if I can dance a step or two."

"That's not dancing," Al said ruefully.

But Walter continued to lift his feet and jiggle them forward and backward in imitation of an act he'd seen.

He was breathless when there was a clumping on the floor that wasn't an echo of any dance step. The landlord below was pounding on the ceiling.

"Let him go to h e double l," Winchell said.

But Mrs. Winschel came home and put a stop to the racket.

"In ten years you could be a dancer," she said. "For now you will go to school."

He looked at her without love in his eyes. His craving for affection had been snuffed out, but his thirst for flattery and appreciation had grown. He would show her.

For a few weeks he sold newspapers on the street corner. A kindly man was impressed by his anxiousness to please. He tipped him—with a pass for the Alhambra Theater.

He had never seen a pass before. Neither had any of the other boys in his class. He showed it off until it was thumb-smudged and tattered.

He lied to his schoolmates, telling them his father was the manager of the Alhambra. When his lie was discovered, he became an object of ridicule.

For three weeks Winchell didn't return to the classroom.

The craving to be more than he is would haunt him all the days of his life.

He continued to practice the amateur dance steps. He got a job as an usher at the Regent Theater, was fired. He applied for a job as usher at the Imperial Theater, a vaudeville house. There was competition for the usher jobs. Everybody wanted to work inside so they could see the stage shows. Winchell withdrew.

He then applied for a job as ticket-taker. There were no competitors for the ticket-taker's job. He got the job.

It was easier when there were no competitors. He had learned a lesson that would stick.

The cashier encouraged him. Her own son worked at the theater too. The son's name was George Jessel.

There was more excitement in the vaudeville house than in the classroom. Finally he stopped attending school altogether.

He was thirteen years old, had progressed as far as 6-B, and was one term behind the normal schedule.

"I was the class dunce," he said later.

For the rest of his life he would be remarkably innocent of book learning.

At the theater he joined up with another usher named Jack Weiner. Jessel joined them and they formed an act called "McKinley, Stanley and Lawrence."

Winchell created the name. He was Stanley. Had he selected to stay with that name, the world would have known him as Walter Stanley.

The act was terrible. Georgie Jessel remembers it with the sentimentality that old vaudevillians attach to their early days.

"Winchell doesn't feel the way I do about it," Jessel admits. "He doesn't have that warm feeling toward the old times that I do."

Winchell was the businessman for the act. The trio were all under fourteen.

Jessel remembers that after a particularly miserable performance, the trio felt they would get sacked.

"Let's counterattack," Winchell suggested.

When the manager came backstage, Winchell didn't wait to be greeted.

"We want more money," he said.

"You stink," the manager said. "The whole act stinks but you especially stink."

Winchell blanched but he didn't change a wrinkle of the scowl on his young face. He had already developed the protective coloration of a hard hide.

"Do we get more money?"

"I'll tell you what I'm going to give you young gentle-men," the manager said slowly. "I'm going to give you an hour to clear out of here to save me the trouble of having you thrown out. The three of you, go home to your mothers."

When the manager left the dressing hall, Winchell turned on Jack Weiner.

"This is your fault," he screamed. "I told you the jokes are lousy."

The jokes included the one about the man who got on the streetcar with his son. When he walked inside after paying only one fare the conductor called him back and said, "What about the boy?"

"He's only four."

"Four!" said the conductor in disbelief. "He looks every bit of eight."

"Can I help it if he worries?" the father said.

Weiner later insisted that Winchell had stolen the jokes from another trio.

"Winchell talked too fast," he said. "He talked us right out of that job."

A few months later Jessel and Winchell got jobs with Gus Edwards's Song Review, a troupe which consisted largely of juvenile talent which somehow managed to evade and avoid schooling.

The hit song of the troupe was "School Days."

Winchell sang and told jokes.

Gus Edwards couldn't decide whether the singing was worse than the joke-telling or the joke-telling worse than the singing. He solved his dilemma by firing Winchell in Providence, Rhode Island.

Winchell hitch-hiked back to New York. Vaudeville was an expanding industry with a large appetite for cheap acts to fill time. Winchell managed to keep employed enough to eat.

At fourteen he got his first attack of "girl trouble." He moved in with a seventeen year old girl whom he'd met backstage at one of the theaters.

In a few weeks she evicted him, because, she said, she wanted to make room for a man.

He was hurt. For awhile he went around carrying a torch. But it flickered and burned out. In a matter of weeks, he had moved in with another young lady and was courting still another on the side.

"I'm a variety man," he boasted to colleagues.

He continued to be a "variety man." Years later when his wife was in a hospital giving birth to a second daughter, he was strolling in Central Park holding hands with a current flame.

3

A Sleuth Burns His Nose

In 1915 Walter Winchell was a raucous, egocentric little vaudevillian who worked hard to amuse audiences that never seemed to like his style.

He'd been spelling his name Winchel when he reached Chicago. There an extra "l" was accidentally added to the program listing. He liked the way his name looked with two "l's" and adopted it.

In Chicago too he experienced his first click as an entertainer. There was a war on in Europe. People were calling sauerkraut "liberty cabbage." Dachshunds were being stoned by angry gangs of hoodlum patriots.

Winchell marched onto the stage carrying an American flag. He held the flag up and, gazing upon it, sang an ode of devotion to "those wonderful American Stars and Stripes."

It would have been treasonable not to applaud that act.

But soon all the second-raters in the vaudeville circuit were taking a cue from the times and guaranteeing themselves applause. Will Mahoney did a tap dance on a xylophone and ended by playing the Star Spangled Banner with his feet. He would step on a button and a large flag would rise.

Others would use the flag as a backdrop or a veil. Soon his spot on the bill had been replaced by a dog act and Winchell was between bookings again. He was being plagued by economic frustration and failure when he enlisted in the Navy.

He slugged it out with the Kaiser from a desk in the New York customs house as a receptionist to the late Rear Admiral Marburg Johnson.

(In World War II he did most of his slugging from table #50 at the Stork Club. The greatest danger he was ever in in either war was from smoking too many cigarettes and eating too much food while he talked.)

There was the quality of a voyeur about Winchell from his boyhood days.

His brother Al remembers that in the tenement as a very young boy, Winchell would try to listen to what was going on in the neighbor's apartment.

"He would hold a glass against the wall and press his ear against it to hear better," Al revealed.

Once he had a pitcher of cold water thrown at him when he tried to peer into the local whore house. He'd been told by his father that that was where "people have babies."

This quality of intrusive snooping was to develop into a multi-million dollar asset.

One day Admiral Johnson and some of his fellow officers were discussing the facts of life as they applied to Naval Officers let loose on women-plentiful Manhattan Island.

At that moment, yeoman Winchell was putting sealing wax on envelopes, a practice commonplace during the first quarter of this century.

A candle was held under a stick of colored wax until enough dripped onto an envelope flap. Then a metal insignia or initial stamp was pressed onto the wax.

The envelope couldn't be opened without breaking the wax seal.

Winchell was sealing the envelopes and then forgot what he was doing as he heard the officers discuss the charms of a young lady who worked in a nearby office.

The young enlisted man leaned forward, unsealed envelope in hand, to hear better what was going on in the next room.

The discussion of the officers was rent by a cry of hideous pain from the next room.

Admiral Johnson and the others kicked over chairs to rush to the rescue.

Yeoman Winchell was jumping up and down and holding his own nose.

"He kept yelling 'Help me, I'm burning, I'm burning,'" Johnson said later, "and sure enough he was. Winchell had become so engrossed in eavesdropping that he had set his own nose afire with the candle."

Johnson turned to an aide. "I can't stand it any longer," he said. "Somebody send this kid to sea."

Winchell was then assigned to routine drilling aboard a ship stationed in the harbor.

It is worth noting that when the story finally caught up with Winchell in his later years, he first denied it and later said that he had been overhearing "top naval secrets."

But to the end Johnson insisted: "The kid's a liar. We were talking about women. He had what you might call a burning curiosity about them."

Discharged from the Navy in 1918, Walter Winchell attempted to return to show business. Vaudeville was going through its golden age and Winchell teamed up with Rita Green, a former partner of his former partner George Jessel.

The act was called Winchell and Green and it played the Pantages circuit and some of the Loew theaters.

It was a talking, singing and dancing act. Winchell did all the talking, keeping up a continuous patter while his partner did a kind of dance to piano accompaniment. His chatter helped to draw attention from his poor footwork, for he had not had any training in real dancing and only could fake a few steps.

The team did fairly well for a while, and then again bookings began to fall off.

Walter Winchell married Rita Green. The act and the marriage began to break up simultaneously in 1920.

Today Rita Green works as a secretary in a law office in Manhattan.

Some years ago she wrote the first part of an autobiography dealing mostly with her life with Winchell.

It never saw printer's ink.

Winchell began paying her $75 a week "living expenses."

He still is paying her.

In 1517 a Roman Catholic priest named Martin Luther nailed his 95 theses to the door of a church in Wittenberg, Germany.

In 1919, Walter Winchell tacked the first copy of his one-man one-copy newspaper to the backstage bulletin board of the Palace Theater in Columbus, Ohio.

Both events were to have far-reaching effects.

The Winchell paper was a daily typewritten affair, written entirely by himself. With a natural-born flair for puns, he called the paper *The News Sense*, which when pronounced would sound like "nuisance."

The small news sheet caused him to become a minor celebrity among the other acts.

Many, but not all of the items revealed little known things of little known consequence.

It told where meals were cheap in town. It revealed that a popular hotel was fumigating its rooms. It told where a dice game was in progress nightly.

But the items in *The News Sense* were not always harmless.

"Which tumbler in the Morrissey Brothers act has tumbled for a restaurant waitress at Larry's Bar? Is it the single one or the one whose wife slaves over a hot scrubbing board in Scranton?" he wrote.

Fortunately for Winchell, both of the Morrissey brothers were courting the same waitress and they beat hell out of each other when the item was tacked on the bulletin board.

Other items in *The News Sense* included bits about somebody secretly trying to grow a moustache, somebody not talking to his manager, and somebody paying a claque to sit in the audience for the matinee to applaud her act so she wouldn't be fired. (She was.)

It was when he wrote "Bill J. and Ernestine O'B. are making whoopie" that he got into his first serious trouble.

Bill J. found him in the wings as Winchell waited for his cue to go on.

"Did you write this?" Bill J. asked, with a misleading grin on his face.

"It's signed Winchell, isn't it? Well, that's me. There's only one of me. I guess you're surprised to see your name—"

It was one of the few sentences Winchell ever left unfinished. Bill J's right fist swung forward in an arc, and Winchell had his first black eye.

One burned nose and one blackened eye were his first payments for being too curious about the private affairs of his fellow men.

But the rewards would grow sweeter as the years rolled by.

4

A Career Is Launched

For a while, Winchell dropped *The News Sense,* but he missed the attention it gave him, and the feeling of importance that went with the attention. He started in again in Buffalo.

When Rita Green left him, he tried to develop a new act. He practiced dancing on roller skates.

No bookings. With no bookings, there was no *News Sense.* Still, he stood around in front of the Palace Theater Building and picked up gossip.

He sent a few items to *Variety* but editor Sime Silverman who later tried to help him, felt at this time that the items were stale. Nor was the information reliable.

Winchell lacked the usual news-gathering background. He had no newspaper training and had never learned that there is a sharp distinction between news and gossip. Gossip becomes news only when it is verified as being real instead of something rumored.

Offended by the *Variety* rejection, Winchell sent the items to *The Billboard. The Billboard* printed them.

Here again he leaned toward gossip. When there were enough little items of chitchat, *The Billboard* published them in a column called "Stage Whispers."

Only the initials W.W. identified the author, and many show folks thought these represented another vaudevillian newsman, Walter Weems.

At the age of twenty-five, Walter Winchell had been in show business twelve years. By all standards including his own, he was a failure. His marriage had failed. His act had failed. He was broke. He was nowhere.

It was four weeks until his next booking and that would pay him $38 a week.

Other out-of-work acts had learned to avoid him so they wouldn't have to listen to long-winded obviously untrue boasts about what he'd told Albee that morning or what Keith promised next month in the way of work. (Keith-Albee was the largest booking agency in the country.)

Winchell was, according to showman Pat Casey who knew him then, "an utterly prosaic bore."

He was standing in front of the Palace Theater with holes in the soles of his shoes when a messenger approached him.

"Are you William Winchell?"

"Walter."

"They want to see you over at the Albee office."

"You tell Albee I want more money," he said in a loud voice so that all might hear. Later he admitted he thought the boy was looking for someone else. "Tell him a hundred a week and second billing or he can make paper airplanes out of the contract."

Puzzled, the boy returned the way he came.

When the attention of the loiterers turned elsewhere, Winchell sidled over to Edward James Smythe.

"Say, Smythe, can you let me have two fish? I left my billfold in my other pants."

Smythe loaned him the two dollars. Smythe, like Winchell, enjoyed playing the role of big shot. He would often lend Winchell a dollar or two though he himself was on a streak of unemployment.

(Years later Smythe became a professional race hate salesman and Winchell was one of the first to attack him. All of which burned Smythe up, and to this day he complains to drinking companions at various bars, "That four-flushin' bum never did pay me back. You'd think he'd pay me back before calling me all of them foul names!")

A couple of days later, Winchell was wandering by the *Variety* office (he'd asked for and been refused a job there) when Glenn Condon called to him from across the street. Condon was editor of the new *Vaudeville News*.

"Walter, why didn't you show at the office when Albee sent for you?"

Winchell gulped. "But I thought . . ."

"It occurred to me you might like to do a little running around for us. You know, picking up the news. You could maybe write a page. The way you used to do that News Sense. But no dirt. We're trying to make friends."

"What's in it?"

"It wouldn't take much time. Say a couple of tens."

"Make it twenty-five?"

"You've just had your first raise."

"But that won't buy me coffee and . . ." he mused to himself.

"It's the best we can do, kiddo. Your choice."

"I'll take it." Winchell brightened. "Say, what about me selling some ads to go with it?"

Condon promised to ask the owner. It was arranged. In a couple of days Winchell had rented a camera from a pawn shop on Ninth Avenue. He planted himself in front of the Palace Theater. He was reporter, advertising manager and chief photographer. The salary was still only $25 a week but he would be paid $3 for each picture the weekly used, and twenty percent of all the advertising revenue he brought in.

Thus it was that he sold puffs. He promised to credit poems or jokes or clever sayings to any and all who would buy an ad.

"It's all the very best publicity," he would say.

For the benefit of future historians, it should be pointed out that *Vaudeville News* was the weekly published by the National Variety Artists.

More important, it should be pointed out that the NVA was then a house "union," owned lock, stock and barrel by the Keith-Albee vaudeville circuit, which was trying to squelch the then aborning AFL union movement among performers.

Vaudeville News was, in short, a publicity club used to clobber any dissent from performers in the E. F. Albee zoo, and to weed out those who showed sympathy toward unionism.

Albee's idea was to starve out of bookings and publicity any who would not bow to his terms.

Winchell was a good flunkey.

He would pick up rumor and hearsay. The innocuous material he would publish in his column. Anything which might help Albee uncover unionism was turned over to Condon for prompt relay to Albee.

"He was good," Condon said. "I found myself trying to hide the fact from Mr. Albee that performers were turning to Winchell's page before reading the Albee editorials."

One of the first ads he sold was to The Tavern at 156 West 48 Street, "a chop house of exceptional merit." Its proprietor was William F. La Hiff. Later, La Hiff would import as his manager a rosy cheeked Philadelphian named Toots Shor.

Winchell seemed taut and self-conscious in his new role as newsman-all-the-time. He was unable to relax. He was highly sensitive and especially upset when a performer refused to take him seriously.

Vaudevillians who were failures in that field very often adjusted to reality by changing their professions. This was done without shame, and a then current piece of repartee concerned the fact that the work was less glamorous but the pay more consistent.

Nevertheless, Winchell gave many people the impression that he was fearful of ribbing.

George Jessel recently mused: "We who were successful had learned to love our audiences. And when we loved 'em, they knew it. It was something you couldn't put your finger on, but they knew it. Walter's trouble was that he didn't like the audience. He was afraid of it and so he wanted to outsmart it, to convince himself he was sharper than they were. He didn't love them and they could sense it."

And yet his new job had its compensations. Vaudeville had never given him the feeling of being "more important" than the audience out front.

Now however he was in a position where he could both help and harm an act, depending on his whim and the willingness of the act to advertise in *Vaudeville News*.

Walter Winchell would never make the mistake of trying to do a soft shoe dance for a living again.

5

June in January

For the first few weeks on *Vaudeville News*, Winchell limited his offerings to factual notices of who was sick, who was playing where, and what acts had changed their acts. He worked day and night trying to outdo the competition of *Variety*.

At this time, Albee was feuding with *Variety* because it had taken the side of the performer. Acts which advertised in *Variety* were blacklisted. The feud lasted two years and very nearly put *Variety* out of business.

It was an item about a dog that brought him back to gossip again.

"We're sorry to learn that Porkchops is sick," he wrote.

He received calls and letters from show business troupers who wanted to know where Porkchops and his master were, and how sick the pooch really was.

From then on Winchell reverted to occasional gossip items. Many of these were designed to flatter those performers who had expressed strong anti-union sentiments.

E. F. Albee was deducting 5% of an act's salary for "bookkeeping." This was apart from any booking commission they had to pay, contributions they had to make, bribes they had to hand out to keep working.

When some acts protested at the 5% deduction for "bookkeeping" by Albee, Albee fired them.

Winchell, knowing where the icing on his cake lay, praised Albee for his "indefatigable fight against the radicals."

Among those who were fired were acts which had toured with Winchell and which considered him their friends.

When they met him on Broadway, they snubbed him. Winchell wrote on his page:

Broadway is a pretty phony avenue. Its honest citizens are in the minority, and a small group they are too.

Two weeks later he told an acquaintance, "I don't care what those cruds say about me. To me it's every man for himself. The other fellow will knife you if you don't cut him up first."

On his page he published a four line verse titled "Broadway."

Every morn I ramble on you.
While the incandescents sleep;
With my troubles I come to you
For I'm one of your black sheep.

Winchell was a sucker for a rumor. Two comedians seeing Winchell drinking coffee in a restaurant, began to talk in loud whispers about "that 17 year old girl at the National Variety Club who was adopting a baby."

Winchell's ears grew.

"Say," he said. "I'm Walter Winchell. I write a page for *Vaudeville News*. Who is that girl you were talking about?"

"Are you the same Winchell who finks for Albee?" one said.

"Let's go, Cecil, this place is polluted," the other said with a wink.

The two left. Winchell spent the whole day trying to learn the name of the girl.

It was after eleven when Winchell finally learned that the girl with a baby in the National Variety Club was June Aster.

It was nearly one o'clock when he managed to slip into the club (against regulations) and rap on her door.

He rapped louder.

Finally, the door swung back a few inches.

"What is it and what do you want?" a sleepy voice asked.

"I'm Walter Winchell of the *Vaudeville News*. I'm here to get a story about you and your baby."

She pulled the door further back. "*You're what?*" she said.

Winchell found himself looking at a long-haired blue-eyed young woman with an expression of angry disbelief on her face. He repeated his mission.

She slammed the door in his face.

He made a hasty exit from the rooming house.

The next morning, bright and early, he was at her door again. The door swung open and a hand reached out to take in the milk bottle.

"Don't go away mad," he said.

The woman behind the door looked just long enough to recognize the intruder. "You're crazy," she said. "Go away or I'll call a cop."

The door slammed again.

Winchell persisted.

"I want to take a picture of you and the baby," he shouted over the transom.

Within a half-hour he had talked his way into taking the picture. An hour later he left. That evening he was back to ask for a date. He got the date.

Like Winchell, June Magee Aster had been a failure as a vaudeville performer. Unlike Winchell, she disliked performing, disliked the spotlight, disliked superficial flattery, and cared little for praise or applause. She was essentially a placid type.

There should have been nothing in common between the two. But perhaps June Aster was intrigued by the sharp-faced fast-talking young man who could be brash, timid and pleading all at the same time. Both June and Walter had blue eyes. She may have liked him for that. Or perhaps she was struck by his trigger-fast talk, with his unusual nervous energy, or with his remarkable assurance of his own destiny.

("I think," the late George M. Cohan once told friends, "that little Walter decided at an early age that he was to be very important. From then on, it was only a matter of finding the method.")

For a long time, June's sister tried to discourage her interest in the sharply dressed young man whose voice seemed to have a frenetic swagger.

But the courtship continued.

It continued past where acquaintances said Winchell would cool off and be on another girlie chase.

A few months later found them living in bliss. June had worn one wedding band and wasn't particularly anxious for another.

In 1923 they were legally married.

So began the marriage which soon leveled off into one of convenience.

An article in Ladies Home Journal would later attribute their "successful" marriage to their never being together long enough to get on each other's nerves.

"In every sense of the word," wrote Parker Morrell, "theirs is a most remarkable union. Temperamentally the two are as completely unlike as Jack Sprat and his wife. Walter is quick, nervous, sentimental and excitable. Mrs. Winchell is calm, easygoing, understanding and tolerant."

One woman was not enough for Winchell's ego, and within a few years he would be off on a series of one man wolf packs in search of willing chorines.

But for the time being, he was happy with his choice.

June Winchell wasn't adopting a baby, as the cafeteria tipsters had wrongly led him to believe. She was caring for the illegitimate baby of a friend, while the friend visited her parents to break the bad news.

Eventually however June did go on an adoption kick. But that came later.

First she bore Walter two daughters. Winchell named the first one Walda. With his expanding ego, he wanted to name the second Walterette. However the second child was named Gloria. She died in 1932.

Walda has done everything she could to lose the given name. She called herself Eileen. She gave herself the stage name of Toni Eden.

In the thirties, June gave birth again, after Winchell had skyrocketed into national prominence.

Winchell was looking for a boy and he wanted to name it Reid Winchell. June would have none of it.

On Broadway, the wags were suggesting that if it were a girl she be named Sue Winchell.

It was a boy and there was strong Broadway sentiment for naming him Lynch Winchell.

The boy was named Walter.

Naturally.

6

The Past That Was Prologue

It is doubtful if Walter Winchell ever considered the *Vaudeville News* more than just a stopping off place.

He returned his rented camera to the Ninth Avenue pawn shop. Then he borrowed a more expensive one from a man named C. Reece Warde. Warde was later to become a Wall Street bucket shop operator who bilked a million or so dollars from his clients.

After Winchell borrowed the camera from Warde, he borrowed Warde's girl friend, a lass named Gertrude. For a while Winchell helped Gertrude keep house, while June kept house all by herself.

Armed with the camera, Winchell would park in front of the Palace Theater and accost the acts as they came down from the many booking agency offices located in the building.

He was fast talking and persuasive. He snooped. He listened. But most of the time he talked.

"Listen, kiddo, how would you like to have your picture in *Vaudeville News?*" he would say.

"Twenty-three skidoo," might be the response.

"This will help you twiddle the gates of fame," he would continue, unabashed. "You know what it means to keep your name before the big shots? Why there was a snake charmer two weeks ago who was flat on her pratt. She was planning to skin her last cobra for soup meat. I ran a photo and a paragraph about her and she's booked solid through March."

Without taking a breath, he would break out a copy of *Vaudeville News* and turn the pages rapidly. "Take a look at some of the names in here, kiddo. This is big time company."

"He had all the manner of a sidewalk pitchman," an actor recalls. "There was nothing gentle about his approach. He was a kind of a pest, and yet you didn't mind him, and if you could spare five or ten dollars you bought his ad and helped him write a couple of sentences about you."

Small, dapper, and incredibly brassy, Winchell managed to badger or browbeat enough of the performers into advertising so that his commissions added to his base salary soon were totalling as high as $67 to $70 a week.

This, in those days, was a considerable amount of money.

But it was the prestige that counted. He became especially proud of the fact that someone chose to nominate him to the general publicity committee of the NVA Sick and Benefit Fund Campaign.

Winchell became clothes conscious.

His wife preferred plain white shirts, but lady friend Gertrude liked sharp plaids and checks. Winchell wore sharp plaids and checks. It was the first time he could afford to buy the clothes he wanted.

He sported a new straw hat one day. When the Palace Theater Building pigeons played an innocent prank on him, soiling and spoiling the hat, he returned it to the Nat Lewis haberdashery and demanded a new one. There was no reason, no logic to his request.

"He just walked in and said, 'Give me a different one for this. Look what happened to it. I'm Winchell of the *Vaudeville News*,'" Nat Lewis recalls.

"We were so amazed that we gave him a new hat. In the long run he was a good walking advertisement. He told everybody that he bought his clothes only at our place."

The next morning, Winchell had the doorman at the Palace take his picture with a theatrical trouper, Anna Chandler.

He arrived at *Vaudeville News* and told editor Condon: "You might file this picture away, boss. You can't ever tell when you might need one of me."

But if he was brash one day, he was timid and inoffensive the next. In the early months he sometimes seemed to have difficulty in developing the rousing braggadocio necessary to attack his sidewalk photographer's assignment.

Then he would sit in a corner of the office glumly sipping his coffee, scratching out little love sonnets to Gertrude, which he would persuade the office boy to deliver in exchange for a pass to the Palace.

His moods were as variable as the weather. One day he would bristle with energy and confidence and the next day he would seem to be wrung out.

However the driving force within him was never completely extinguished. On occasion he would sit alone in the office through the night trying to perfect a ragged verse of doggerel.

More than a year had passed since his arrival on *Vaudville News* and certain changes were taking place both in policy and personnel.

A new editor had taken Condon's job. Winchell became fretful that he too would be replaced "by some creep who'll settle for a flat thirty bucks a week."

The fear became a kind of obsession and for days on end he couldn't keep any food on his stomach. He subsisted on ice cream sodas and cigarettes, smoking two and three packs of cigarettes a day. He could guzzle four ice cream sodas at a sitting, and often did.

When it appeared that his job was tentatively secure, he resumed his work with a new wilder vigor.

By this time Gertrude had gone back to C. Reece

Warde, and had taken his camera with her. Winchell concentrated on gags and puns and idle news items. His ability to secure new ads even without a camera had become ingrained.

"I can sell Fatima cigarettes to a dead Egyptian," he boasted.

When one actor protested that he was broke and couldn't afford to pay for an ad at the moment, Winchell retorted simply: "Hock something. There's a pawn shop on forty-sixth. I'll walk you over there."

And he walked over, assuring the actor that the comforts derived from a stick pin or a pocket watch were nothing as compared to the importance of having one's name in the right place at the proper time.

But when the new editor, R. B. Hennessy suggested that Winchell give up the news page and concentrate only on selling ads, Winchell stamped out of the office muttering dark and evil things such as that he would quit *Vaudeville News.*

Nevertheless, opportunity wasn't bobbing its bobbed head that season. Winchell continued to work for *Vaudeville News* for almost another year.

When he finally departed from *Vaudeville News,* that paper mentioned him no more, except to remark once that he had been its first columnist.

On the floor in the front part of the *Vaudeville News* office, an office boy pasted a small sign above the spittoon.

"Walter Winchell spit here," he wrote.

7

Winchell Gets a Job

Fulton Oursler, a prominent atheist of the 1920's, wrote booklets pointing up some of the fallacies and inconsistencies in the Bible for E. Haldeman-Julius. Oursler eventually turned to religion which he found much more profitable, for where the Haldeman-Julius "Little Blue Books" each brought him all of $50 or $100 flat payment, books on religion brought him an income easily exceeding $500,000 during three years in the late 40's.

Oursler is dead now, and E. Haldeman-Julius drowned himself in his private swimming pool after his conviction for income tax evasion.

E. Haldeman-Julius brought culture to millions of people with his 5¢ "Little Blue Books."

Oursler brought Winchell into flower.

It is not remarkable that Oursler's appreciation of Winchell stemmed from the latter's errors in fact.

Oursler was lunching with some show people at Bleeck's Artists and Writers Club when the show folks at his table got into an angry argument about the untruths they had discovered in Winchell's column about themselves.

Now, oddly, the errors were not errors in gossip, but rather errors because Winchell had been sloppy about interpreting news of a booking date.

Oursler listened, intrigued. He was then working on a study of the Bible. He believed then that part of the reason the Bible had survived so long was because it offered so many obvious contradictions, so much sloppy reportage.

He was naturally attracted to the Winchell column in *Vaudeville News.*

"There was nothing exciting in it," he later said. "The writing was nothing to write to Chaucer about. But what he was saying didn't appeal to me while the way he was saying it did. It was personal. It was intimate."

Oursler sensed in Winchell a fondness for Broadway that was lacking in some of the other routine chatter columns.

As proof, he would show people a poem he carried about with him which he'd clipped from a Winchell column in the *Vaudeville News* of December 22, 1922. It was titled "Your Broadway and Mine"—later to become a title for some Winchell columns.

This was the poem:

> Broadway bred me, Broadway fed me,
> Broadway led me—
> to a goal.
> Broadway boo'd me and pooh-pooh'd me,
> Disapproved me—
> in the role.
> Broadway scared me, Broadway dared me
> It prepared me—
> to be shrewd
> Broadway cursed me, Broadway nursed me,
> It rehearsed me—
> how to brood.
> Broadway canned me, Broadway banned me,
> Broadway panned me—
> and my muse
> Broadway slammed me, rammed and damned me
> Broadway taught me,
> how to lose
> Broadway ruled me, Broadway fooled me,
> Broadway schooled me
> how to cry
> Though it trumped me, bumped and dumped me,
> Broadway's where I want to die.

"It was the same quality of corn that I find in Edgar A. Guest," Oursler remarked later. "It was trash. It was awful. But it had appeal for that vast audience of semiliterates who liked awful trash.

"I wrote some of it myself and sent it to him and he rejected it which showed at least that he had some taste. When I went to pick the poems up, he acted happy to see me, and in a matter of minutes was confiding to me about all the juiciest gossip. He seemed to know what was going on in everybody's bedroom.

"I found his dissertations fascinating. I found myself sending him more putrid poetry just to have the chance to pick it up and listen to his chatter. I picked up enough dirt on each visit to become the star attraction at a month of lunches with my friends."

Oursler represented Bernarr Macfadden as supervising editor when physical culturist Macfadden decided to launch a newspaper. The paper was tentatively named "The Truth."

The title seemed to leave business manager John Cook in a stupor. Cook warned that the intention to stalk the truth and publish it every day would result in nothing but disaster. The name was changed to *The Evening Graphic*.

But disaster came onto the paper in the form of Walter Winchell, who, said Oursler, knew something about show people and ought to conduct the theatrical section. Oursler made his sentiments known to Emile Gauvreau, the editor.

Gauvreau, happy to please his superior, hired Winchell at $100 a week. Winchell was to receive in addition, 15% of the advertising revenue he brought in. He was to turn news tips over to Gauvreau. And he would be permitted to write his jokes and gags and miscellany into a column.

The *Graphic* began publishing on September 15, 1924.

Once again, Winchell found himself doing well by

selling ads and giving the advertisers plugs in his column as a "bonus."

His jobs were many. He was drama critic, movie editor, columnist, theatrical ad salesman, and general office boy for Gauvreau.

His material was conservative when compared to the general content of the *Graphic* which carried such headlines as:

I HATED MY MOTHER
SO I KILLED HER

and

SIN BROUGHT ME MONEY
BUT NO TRUE HAPPINESS

The circulation of the *Graphic* had climbed to 400,000 and dipped to 83,000 all within its first two weeks.

One of Winchell's co-workers from the early *Graphic* days remembers him as a sharp fellow, quick with a retort. "We thought he was a nice enough guy and he worked hard like the rest of us. He had a lean hungry look but he was young and he was so ambitious that when you watched him crouched tensely before his typewriter, he reminded you of a five pound sack into which ten pounds of humus had been pounded. You looked at him and expected something to give at any moment."

Winchell was on the *Graphic* for almost a year before he wrote his first pure gossip column.

Until then he raced around to beg ads from theater managers, to pick up little items of news, to pour through anthologies in search of gags that he could up-date and use in his column of odds and ends.

He took to hanging around the *Variety* offices on 46th Street where some of the *Variety* reporters felt sorry for him and allowed him to be a scavenger for the cast out material which lacked trade significance but might interest the *Graphic* public.

Thus, *Variety* might report in its columns that Melville Mumford had joined the cast of "The Mighty Blue." But it wouldn't mention that Mumford was one of Lillian Russell's ex-husbands.

The last choice morsel was thrown to Winchell. It was considered garbage at *Variety*. It was considered garbage at the *Graphic* where Winchell used it.

But it was garbage with a strange odor. It was the kind of garbage which would blossom into the multi-million dollar movie fan magazine industry. It was the kind of garbage which would sprout Louella Parsons and Hedda Hopper and Jimmy Fidler.

It was garbage with a personal flavor.

It became more personal when Winchell told the city desk man that maybe a certain separated couple would get together again. The couple were Frank Tinney and Imogene Wilson, celebrities of that era about whose private lives there had already been much public scandal.

Winchell told the city desk man the item he'd written out in pencil was a "hot" one. The item said the Tinney's might move into the same hotel room within a week.

"Nobody cares," said the city desk man, and he tossed the item in the waste basket.

Winchell cared. He cared even more when during the following week the couple did reconcile and a rival newspaper published the story first.

This was the scandal which would launch Winchell on the road to becoming a national institution.

On the following Monday he turned in a column with various gossip and personal items he had picked up on his rounds. It was crowded with the names of important show people. The items were a mixture of fact, guess and speculation.

The column created an immediate stir among Broadway people.

At La Hiff's Tavern, Winchell assured the patrons that all gossip items given to him would receive his personal consideration.

"I'm Winchell," he told the bartender. "I do that Monday column in the *Graphic*."

"I'm Winchell," he told actor Claude Cooper, just before asking for a free pass to Cooper's show. "You probably read my stuff in the *Graphic*."

"I'm Winchell," he told whoever would listen. "I write that column."

Bishop Fulton J. Sheen has never revealed whether Fulton Oursler, at his deathbed confession, apologized to his God for giving Winchell to the world.

8

The Arc Widens

The white faced young man stood in front of the West Forty-Eighth Street saloon impatiently rocking the carriage to and fro.

Walter Winchell looked down at his daughter and then at the clock in the window of the Postal Telegraph office across the street.

The young man was now earning more than two hundred dollars a week. His jottings had commanded the attention of an audience so large that the *Graphic* had promised him a raise for Christmas.

Rocking a baby was no job for an important newspaperman.

Though it was early in the day, a few newsmen were dropping into the tavern, and the young man seemed embarrassed with his task.

His was the only baby carriage on the street.

"You keep that carriage in front," tavern owner Billy La Hiff had told him. "It makes the joint look respectable."

From the Broadway end of the street, two dapper men started down toward him.

They were on their way to Sixth Avenue.

As they neared the man with the baby carriage, Winchell waved gallantly at Sime Silverman, publisher and editor of *Variety*.

"Hello, Mr. Silverman. Did you see Monday's column? I used that material."

"I saw it, Walter."

Sime Silverman introduced his companion.

The three men talked about a current much-publicized murder case. The third man started to express an opinion when Winchell cut in.

"Say have you fellows seen these?"

He pulled out his wallet and produced soiled strips of a newspaper article by Robert Benchley. The article acclaimed him as a new phenomenon in Americana.

The two men read the column and nodded approvingly.

"You keep at it, Walter. You're doing fine."

"Thanks, Sime."

The young man placed the clippings in his wallet with affectionate care as the two men walked on. Then he resumed his nervous rocking of the carriage.

"So that's Winchell," Damon Runyon said. After a few more steps he spoke again: "I don't like him."

"This the first time you met him?"

"Yep."

"He'll grow on you. He's clever with a pun. He's fast."

"I don't like ostentation," Runyon said. "He's a show off."

"What about you, bragging all the time about your expensive clothes."

Runyon laughed. "I'm mortal. I don't practice everything I preach."

"What do you think of his column?"

"Kid stuff. I don't understand why adults read it."

Silverman shook his head in disagreement. "You're wrong, Runyon. They're reading it. The kid's going places. It's supposed to be a secret but he's also writing the Beau Broadway column now for the *Morning Telegraph*."

"I know," said Runyon. "Some secret. He's told half the town."

The two men turned on Sixth Avenue.

"Hellinger is a better writer," Runyon remarked. "So is Brisbane."

"So are you," said Silverman. "But he's new. He's vogue."

"Gossip is for women," Runyon insisted. "I used to think Winchell was a woman."

Silverman chuckled. "No woman would have his nerve."

"How do you mean?" Runyon said.

The men walked on in silence. Finally Silverman explained: "He's stealing. He steals phrases from Tommy Gray and ideas from McIntyre. He's swiping Jack Conway's epigrams and Johnny O'Connor's salt."

"I steal," Runyon said. "I steal from the classics."

"Good, so you're brothers under the skin," Silverman said dryly.

"Let me choose my brothers," Runyon said. "I still don't like him."

"You will," Silverman said.

Silverman didn't live to see his prophecy come true. He died a few years later. When he died, he himself was no longer on speaking terms with Walter Winchell.

9

A Giant Step

The *New York Evening Graphic* had its offices at 350 Hudson Street. Its slogan was "Nothing But The Truth."

On its editorial page, it boasted of its "Bureau of Fairness and Truth."

"All complaints of inaccuracy and unfairness in any column of the *Graphic* should be addressed to this bureau. Each such complaint will be carefully investigated, and if discovered to be well-founded, prompt prominent and thorough redress will be made."

Editor Emile Gauvreau denied that the box was written especially to placate complaints about the Winchell column, and Gauvreau is an honorable man.

More, the Winchell gossip column appeared only on Mondays. On other days of the week, he would buttress his byline with press agent reports on what stars were going into what shows and what silent movies were opening next week.

But the Monday column was the thing.

A breathless audience could learn that "Five pounds of matzoths were expressed to F. Ziegfeld in Florida."

That Ziegfeld was in Hawthorne, New Jersey at the time didn't detract from the glamour of the item for the growing thousands who read widely and eagerly about the ushering in of America's feverishly gay jazz age.

Somehow newspaper readers were given the feeling that they were being fed inside information by an insider. Psychiatrists would have to determine what peculiar satisfaction might be gained from knowing that five pounds of matzoths or even a loaf of pumpernickel bread was being shipped to Ziegfeld.

It might also be worth determining how a reader's pleasures are enhanced by knowing that a particular movie actress was seen with a not-so-particular booking agent in a speakeasy.

It was the blind items which caused the most stir and evoked the most comment.

A song publisher was able to get Winchell to write that "I Can't Give you Anything But Love" is a sizzling foxtrot . . . by also giving him an item like this:

"What ticket speculator dropped $17,000 in a dice house the other morning?"

That was a fair question. No names. No clues. Just a question. Now, in truth, it was not necessary for anyone to have dropped $17,000 in a dice game.

$17,000 was a lot of money in those days. People who earned only $17 a week got a morbid pleasure thinking about $17,000. There was something wonderful and something terrible about somebody losing $17,000 in a dice game.

Did Winchell identify Emile Zola as a woman? Well, most of his readers didn't know any better anyway.

And when he asked: "Which of the two prominent theatrical advertising agencies will lay an egg shortly?" perhaps he was only looking for an answer.

His romance items were so preposterous that on May 14, 1928, a wag actually got him to use an item saying that "A. Woollcott is that way over Lizzie Borden."

Now Woollcott was known not to have much to do with women, and Lizzie Borden was a notorious murderess from Massachusetts who had slain her mother and father with an axe.

Winchell knew who Woollcott was. But when asked if he knew who Lizzie Borden was, he told a Billboard reporter in deadly seriousness, "Oh, she's a local kid. I've seen her around."

Winchell dished out plenty of dirt. "Nat Goodwin's fourth divorce has not depressed him. A new leading lady is admirably eligible for matrimony. Ho! Ho!"

Goodwin hadn't secured his fourth divorce, but who can say the item didn't hurry it along.

Winchell had an insatiable hunger for jokes and witty sayings.

One evening at the *Graphic* he heard radio columnist Jerry Wald tell an angry press agent that he could go to hell. "The cemeteries are filled with people who thought the world couldn't get along without them," Wald said.

Winchell used the quote and credited it to Mayor Jimmy Walker.

The next day Wald approached Winchell's desk.

"Hey, Winch," the brash Wald said. "What's the idea of this crack about the cemeteries—"

"Look, kid," Winchell cut in. "You're not somebody worth quoting yet. You should be glad you said something worth quoting. But people don't know you and they know Jimmy Walker."

Wald scratched his head, suddenly unable to say what was on his mind.

"Another thing," Winchell continued, "you're making a mistake with that column of yours. Stop saying nice things about everybody. Nobody'll read you except maybe the mugg you're writing about. Call him an S.O.B. and everybody will read you."

"Thanks for the advice, Winch," said Wald walking away.

"But that crack about the cemeteries. Walker didn't say it and neither did I. It's practically a classic. R. C. O'Brien said it."

Winchell never bothered to print a corrected credit.

However, Wald took Winchell's advice. A few weeks later he delivered below-the-belt attacks on Kate Smith. He wrote snide reviews of Rudy Vallee. In a short time his column was receiving plenty of attention.

Later he became a Hollywood producer and is generally considered to have been the prototype for Sammy in Budd Schulberg's "What Makes Sammy Run?"

Winchell too was getting more and more attention.

He had become friendly with a bootlegger named Sherman Billingsley. Billingsley had served three months and twenty days in the Federal penitentiary at Leavenworth and was once again a front man for the mobs.

Billingsley introduced Winchell to various hoodlums, and gave him tips.

In the gang-business world of today, gangsters have assumed a facade of respectable operations. One of the most important diamond merchants is also the banker for many of the most important gang operations. He has been successful in keeping his name completely out of the limelight, and was not mentioned even once in the recent Kefauver crime investigations, though he is considered far more important than a Frank Costello or a Joe Adonis.

But in the late twenties, it was considered good publicity for a rum runner or a professional killer to get his name in Winchell's column. It meant he'd arrived socially.

In among such social items as one about "Frank Yale is putting the finger on a certain judge," Winchell would also play the role of a tout.

On May 14, 1928, he wrote:

The current tip on the market is Industrial Alcohol and Corn Products Company stock.

On June 11, he tipped off his readers:

The mob is buying Consolidated Retail.

For those who weren't interested in stock tips, there were more blind item puzzles, such as:

What femme movie critic stole a banker from his invalid wife?

That one appeared on June 25, 1928. Twenty-five years later, nobody has answered the question.

But twenty-five years ago, radio commentator John

B. Kennedy credited Winchell with "an amazing degree of penetration and accuracy."

Kennedy later admitted he didn't read Winchell too often and had made no check on the accuracy of a Winchell column.

However he was correct in his appraisal that "this pale determined young man . . . is chief among the fast-thinking, fast-talking, fast-forgotten chroniclers of the names that go up in lights and come down in laughter."

"One day he was a nobody," said Broadway ticket broker Dave Goldberg, "and the next time you looked, everybody was reading his column and around Broadway you had to decide whether to fear him or favor him."

Emile Gauvreau in his "My Last Million Readers" described Winchell as "a hunched figure with a white lean face of deceptive humility, looking up occasionally, startled. He pecked a typewriter, nervously, with a frenzied determination, but from the machine, a form of gossip was beginning to appear which he himself never dreamed could be accorded the benediction of print in a daily paper. When his column, 'Your Broadway and Mine' became the talk of the town, no vestige of humility remained in him."

At this time, Winchell the Oracle made his appearance. "James J. Walker of St. Luke's Place has no intention of running for Mayor of New York again . . ." Winchell wrote on May 7, 1928.

A short time later Walker announced that he would run again. Winchell was wrong again. Walker ran and won.

On November 5th of that year he wrote:

A 'rumor' has Herbert Bayard Swope heading Radio Corp.

Winchell had thus begun to protect himself. If Swope didn't head Radio Corp., (and he didn't) Winchell could always say: "I didn't say he would. I said there was rumor that he would."

On the other hand, if Swope did get the job, Winchell would mention it in his column by writing something like this:

H. B. Swope got that Radio Corp. presidency as we said he would last Nov 5th.

Newspapermen will of course recognize in this example, the point at which Winchell was no longer a newspaperman. A professional newsman would have called Swope to check the truth, if any, of the rumor.

There were many ways to hedge.

A. Brisbane, the Park Rowgue, will definitely retire in June, we are unreliably informed.

This was a partly accurate one, in that Brisbane didn't retire. Winchell *was* "unreliably" informed.

Once in a while, but rarely, Winchell would retract one of his wrong items: " 'Skeets' Miller, who 'made' Floyd Gibbons' death cave, was not fired by the *World*, but shelved it for voice culture . . . Excuseit-please . . ." he wrote.

But to avoid the unpleasantness connected with his having to apologize, Winchell drew more and more upon the so-called blind items, the bits of scandal with no names attached.

With a blind item it was possible to libel without much fear of legal retaliation, for although a blind item could be shown to be libelous if the public pretty much recognized the unnamed parties referred to, still many people have a reluctance to say, "I'm the guy in the item where he doesn't name the guy."

By mixing this blend of dirt with a certain quantity of innocent chatter, some brilliant wisecracks, and some of the worst poems ever to appear in public print, Winchell continued to accumulate readers.

"It may be froth, every bit of it, but the world is fond of it," Walter Winchell has said of his column.

The world may not have been fond of it. Most of the world didn't even know about it. But that part of the world which did, certainly were becoming fanatics.

10

The Die Is Cast

The publishers of the Readers Guide to Periodical Literature may have been totally unaware of the existence of Walter Winchell during the mid-twenties.

The Readers Guides for 1924, 1925 and 1926, list, among important contributions to American culture, an article on "Atoms and Isomorphism" by Alexander Newton Winchell.

Cora Marguerita Winchell was listed for her article "Home Economics at the Crossroad."

The only other Winchells mentioned were Jesse A. and Alida Fairbanks Winchell for their article "What Vermont Parents Think of Home Economics."

Nor did the poetry journals of the day heap laurels on the bard of Broadway for his verse.

Much of it that he published was written by others, though he took full credit for all of it.

One amateur poet wrote a poem which oddly enough expressed the attitude most people who knew Winchell took toward him. Winchell had published it in his column in *Vaudeville News* and he published it again in the *Graphic* on September 19, 1924.

You've Met Him

I have a certain touchy chap in mind,
Whose sensitiveness gives my nerves the jump;
If jokingly I call him names unkind,
He takes me serious, the dawgawn chump!

I've learned I cannot kid him; it offends,
It hurts his tender feelings if I do;
It's just as well that we're no longer friends,
This yap, who seemed a pebble in my shoe.

His column had begun to read like a snappy guide to America's bedroom fortunes.

Frederick Lundberg described Winchell's column in these words: "His writings concern only the boudoir and the bordello. His preoccupation with seduction, wooing, fornication, copulation, conception, pregnancy, parturition, adultery and perversion is pursued out of a spirit of pure malice and vindictiveness."

The weekly column blossomed into a daily, although the material Winchell thought best he saved for the Monday gossip edition.

Broadway was a big place. The street itself is the second longest metropolitan thoroughfare in the nation, taking place position only to Chicago's Halsted Street.

Broadway trails from the lowest strip of Manhattan island to the city limits of Yonkers and beyond.

But for Walter Winchell it began at Times Square and ended at Fifty-Seventh Street.

Winchell had already begun to depend for most of his material on the expanding army of press agents.

However he would spend afternoons and evenings pacing from street to street stopping every familiar face with the familiar question, "What's new? You know anything?"

He would hurry from speakeasy to speakeasy and once inside one of them, would grab people by their arms or coat lapels and say, "Got an item?" or plead, "Aw come on, gimme a gag."

If he was told something, more often than not he would publish it without stopping to determine whether it was true.

Many a character assassin got in his licks through the Winchell column. Occasionally he would try to weed the

consistently wrong tipsters from his congregation of in-
formers.

Many show business wits also fed him with cute
mouthings. If a gag was making the rounds, the vaudevillian who could get his name associated with it first in
Winchell's column could claim some sort of illegitimate
father's privilege for it.

By the time he was thirty years old, Walter Winchell
had become a case hardened youth whose words were
swords and hammers and whose quips often seemed
twisted from barbed wire and dipped in acid.

He was unlike any of the columnists who had
gone before. Benjamin Franklin was the first American
columnist. Others closer to being contemporaries of
Winchell were Eugene Field, Ambrose Bierce and Chris-
topher Morley.

He had only to look about him to see columnists like
Arthur Brisbane, Will Rogers and O. O. McIntyre for
examples of men who were earning more money with
their columns.

(This didn't stop him from claiming in his column that
he was the highest paid newspaper columnist. He just
ignored the others in his reckoning.)

But Winchelliana was already on its way to becoming
a place all its own.

His orange juice gulch and mazda lane reports continued to spawn talk, and the more he was talked about,
the better he liked it.

He was trying desperately to make his column the
castle for smart cracks, clever lines, pert remarks. His
own quips always reflected a hard-boiled attitude toward life, toward women, toward money. He was super-
cilious and superficial and yet at the same time gave his
readers a feeling that they were going deep into the private thoughts, moods and acts of their favorite celebrities.

It became obvious that he never rested. The way
he spiced every confidence with a stream of dots . . .

showed how breathless he was . . . how anxious to get
on to the next seduction . . . the next genuflection to
divorce . . . the next secret come-together of lovers
. . . the next birth . . . the next forecast of death or
who was wearing a size-larger hat.

Readers came away from his column with a feeling
that he was everywhere. He slept in the wing of the Empire Theater with one eye open. At the same time he was
on Fifth Avenue spotting celebrities. He saw all the movies and all the plays and listened to all the new phono-
graph recordings. He tore through all the new books
and magazines, and had dictaphones in the boudoirs
of all famous people. He was a fly at the circus and a
cockroach in a ticker tape machine who could see the
quotations before they came pouring out for the normal human eye.

Even his errors were becoming amazing. He had dead
men getting married. Not knowing that she was in her
early eighties, he announced that a legendary vaudeville
trouper was about to become a mother.

You could have choked him with his errors—if you
could have caught up with him.

The trick was to catch him.

He was becoming increasingly informative to those
who didn't care whether their information was correct
or not as long as it had a confidential flavor.

Other columnists had earned tons of bread and butter
and carloads of bootleg liquor writing about people, but
none had made a specialty of seeming to eavesdrop
everywhere.

He was impudent in his pretense of being familiar
with all the so-called "big shots."

He mentioned that a hotel owner used linens he'd
stolen from a rival hotel. He hinted that a millionaire's
son was being sent to prostitute row in order to discourage homosexual tendencies. He quoted the price of
opium pipes in Chinatown.

"Edna St. Vincent Millay, the love poem writer, just

bought a new set of store teeth," he wrote breathlessly.

Each morning he would make a dramatic entrance into the editorial section of the *Graphic*. He strutted and bowed, he shouted for a copy boy, he did everything but a back double-flip somersault to attract attention.

He would turn the column in and then regally depart, bound for the enchanted Broadway arena. There, stretching out before him he could see or smell the green pastures of scandal which was not quite defamation.

He had become a whole new Winchell ever since his meeting with press agent Irving Hoffman in 1926.

It was Hoffman who tutored Winchell in the ways of libel. It was Hoffman who invented the language which permitted Winchell to tread the paths of intrusive reporting without running into law suits.

For instance, it would have been dangerous and subject to serious recovery of damages if Winchell had written that a couple "is about to be divorced"—when they weren't. Hoffman created the phrase "on the verge." Winchell used it fully and fearlessly, confident that the courts would consider the insinuating words "on the verge" to be legally meaningless.

Hoffman translated Winchell's fondness for phonetics into invented spellings like phlicker, phamous phinancier, phfft, and moom pitcher.

Hoffman was only one of many press agents in Winchell's stable, but for twenty-five years he would be the most important one.

Winchell was aware of his own abysmal lack of education. He found in Hoffman a man of rapier wit—but more important, a man whose learning compensated for his own lack of the stuff.

Some Winchell detractors who give him little other credit, do give him credit for recognizing and harnessing the talents of Hoffman.

One morning, Winchell hurried into the office of the *Graphic* without the bother of a grand entrance.

He approached William E. Robinson, the *Graphic's* president. "Say I'd like you to print this for me. I can pay you back, you know, by writing you up in the column."

(It had become "*the* column," not merely "my column." Everybody was expected to understand that there was only one column and Walter Winchell was its prophet.)

What he wanted Robinson to print was this testimonial about Winchell.

"There's one thing I like most about Walter Winchell's reporting," says a very famous newspaperman. "I like his attitude. He positively leans over backward to be fair and square. I've been reading him since he began and the thing that strikes me most forcibly is that he is so reasonable, so straightforward. He makes statements of facts. There's plenty of sensation in his column but nothing that's hard to follow. I can read Winchell three times a day and never get bored with him."

"Who wrote this damned thing?" Robinson asked in disbelief.

"Are you going to print it?"

"Who wrote it?"

"What's the diff. Let's say my mother wrote it. You print it. If you need a picture of me, I'll get you one."

When Robinson failed to publish the self-praise, Winchell was heard to tell various members of the staff, "I'll take care of him."

(It is not clearly known how Winchell "took care of" Robinson. Today William E. Robinson is the publisher of the *New York Herald Tribune*. He spends his spare hours golfing with President Eisenhower.)

Shortly after this incident, someone accosted Winchell at Texas Guinan's speakeasy, and complained about a nasty item in the column. Winchell replied, "Listen, kid,

I'll admit it wasn't nice of me but around this street they know I'm no good and they like me just the same. That's friendship."

"I like a fair fighter," he wrote in his column on the following Monday.

He haunted the lairs of spurious gayety, writing about them so that they seemed like Babylon revisited, but the tired clothing workers on their way to and from a ten hour day liked to read about the doings of gangsters and dolls and the misdoings of actors and politicians.

Other men had been satirists of the going-to-hell civilization, but Winchell was taking it seriously.

They tittered when he wrote about William Randolph Hearst's mistress as a "keptive."

They felt superior when he mentioned that John Barrymore was addicted to "booze and boozums."

They were part of a secret clan when told that Rudolph Valentino was "that way about men."

The blackmail spirit flowed through Winchell's veins. He wanted always to know what he could "get" on the other fellow.

"What do you know about him?" he would ask someone he was talking to, whenever another person passed by without according him respectful treatment. "Is he doing something he ought to be ashamed of?"

He reflected his own feelings about Broadway when he wrote:

This street is not as gay as its bright bulbs would indicate. It's rather a glum place for most of its alleged butterflies. It is vicious, merciless, selfish and treacherous.

Reading the last sentence aloud at a Lambs' Club Gambol, Al Jolson remarked: "There goes Walter talking about himself again."

Later, Jolson was to punch Winchell in the eye because of a smart-alec line in the column about Ruby Keeler, who at the time was Jolson's wife.

11

Winchell and the Law

Gene Fowler in his "The Great Mouthpiece" described the time Little Billy, the famous Lilliputian actor, visited the Criminal Courts building in the company of the editor of the *Morning Telegraph*, Johnny O'Connor.

O'Connor explained that Little Billy had an underworld complex and was anxious to meet a few criminals. "I took him to see some gorillas," O'Connor said, "but he wouldn't believe they were the real McCoy."

"You've been kidding me," said Little Billy. "I want to see *killers*, like you read about in the papers."

Hearing that O'Connor was going to meet a killer up for the death sentence, Little Billy exclaimed: "Gee, that's swell! Could I get a knock-down to him?"

When it was arranged and the killer was pointed out to Little Billy, the Lilliputian was jubilant. "Oh, boy!" said Little Billy, "This is the *life!* I wonder if I could shake hands with him?"

When introduced, Billy asked, "How does it feel to be like you?"

The killer looked down at the questioner. "Well, little pal," said he, "it feels swell. Yes, pal, it feels swell."

"Gee, but you're some man," Billy said.

Winchell has been an admirer of gangsters since the beginning of his column days.

Their fascination for him could be described as at least equal to that of Little Billy. Until now he has not deviated in his hero-worship of law-breakers, hoodlums and racketeers.

From his earliest column days he was a sycophant who fawned upon the gang leaders, who flattered them with favorable mentions in his column, who tried in every conceivable manner to cajole some measure of friendship from them.

It was as if he lacked inner strength and wanted in some way to associate himself with what he felt was the strength of the gangsters.

In 1952, shortly before gangster Frank Costello went to the penitentiary for, of all things, contempt of Congress, Winchell was able to interview Costello for International News Service, the Hearst-owned press association.

The interview read much like Little Billy saying to the killer, "Gee, but you're some man."

It seemed so foolish that some newspapers including the Miami Daily News published satires of the interview. Winchell had pictured Costello as an altruistic businessman caught in the grips of malicious politicians. The followup was that for one of the few times in his career, Winchell wrote a series of columns trying to justify himself.

In his earliest days, Winchell was introduced to Owney Madden. He tried to spend as much time as he could with Madden. He window-shopped with him, picked up his dates in a cab, and gave Madden the run of the Winchell column for planting items designed to promote Madden's enterprises.

At the *Graphic* office he would crow, "I was with Madden today. He thinks . . ."

For a while Winchell was so proud of his friendship with Madden that the columnist seemed to have no opinions of his own. Even in a conversation about the weather, Winchell would work Madden's name into the talk.

It was a bleak day for Walter Winchell when he found

Madden in the lobby of the old Waldorf-Astoria, surrounded by his bodyguards, and muttering about "the
God-damned newspapermen in this town."

"Owney, what's the matter?" Winchell pleaded.
"What's troubling you?"

"It isn't you, Walter," Madden assured the columnist,
who then took a long deep breath of relief.

Madden then explained that the *New York Herald-
Tribune* was refusing to accord Madden the honors due
a gentleman of America's new jazz society. Every time
Madden's name appeared in the *Tribune,* the *Trib* would
also mention his imprisonment for homicide.

It was bad for Madden's social aspirations.

Winchell promptly visited the city editor of the *Tribune* to try to persuade him not to mention the homicide
in connection with Madden.

Madden was so pleased that he gave Winchell a
$2,000 Stutz, in appreciation.

This information was widely circulated, and embarrassed Winchell into later insisting he had paid for the
car. He didn't have a cancelled check to prove it but he
insisted he paid "in cash."

There was much comfort for Winchell in knowing the
gang chieftains. He made it a policy to seek out gam-
blers, hoods, bookmakers, and whore house madams.

The pale, seemingly bloodless Winchell had the
underworld connections backfire on occasion, and the
occasions frightened him half to death, according to ob-
servers.

On his speakeasy beat was the establishment presided
over by vivacious, sharp-tongued attractive Texas Guinan.

Guinan would humor Winchell, give him the best
table, and offer him the best bathtub gin. He always
refused the liquor, saying, "When you drink it, baby,
then I'll drink it."

Guinan would also provide Winchell with wisecracks
and tips.

It was on a windy evening in November when Guinan showed Winchell an advance copy of *Broadway Brevities*, a weekly tabloid which had become popular with the night spot set.

With a pencil she had circled an item which said: "Mr. Vincent Coll and his associates received $50,000 to rid Saratoga Springs of an obnoxious Chicago gang that infested that resort last summer. New York papers please copy."

Winchell copied. Without credit.

In February he also read an item in *Broadway Brevities* which reported: "That Chicago gang is importing its own crew to New York to shoot it out with V. Coll and associates. There probably isn't anything to the rumor that all concerned are extensions of the "Dutch" Schultz activity. By the way, whatever happened to Owney's brother Frank?"

As was not unusual for him, when he lifted the item Winchell found it necessary to exaggerate it to give it real "Winchell significance."

Thus he reported:

Five planes brought dozens of machine gats from Chicago, Friday to combat the Town's Capone. Local banditti have made one hotel a virtual arsenal and several hot-spots are ditto because Master Coll is giving them a headache . . .

Winchell knew that *Brevities* had been following the career of Vincent Coll, known also as "Mad Dog Coll." That paper seemed to know more about the activities of the Coll man than the police who feared him.

So it was that Winchell, sensing a good thing, lifted freely and without apologies.

The second item appeared in his column on a night in February which, though not cold for February, was to give Winchell a terrible chill.

About an hour after the column hit the midtown newsstands, Coll was machine-gunned to death in a telephone booth at the Cornish Arms Hotel on West 23rd Street.

Winchell was on the editorial floor of the *Graphic* when the news came through.

He became hysterical. He grabbed a fellow-worker and screamed at him, "They're putting me on the spot. What can I do?"

What he did, finally, was to call Owney Madden. Madden told him he would be given a reprieve. Winchell refused to leave the building until a Madden gunman was sent to guard him. The gunman remained with him for several days.

Shortly after that he had a nervous breakdown, one of his three most famous breakdowns. He retired from the paper for six weeks.

When he returned and Arthur Brisbane asked him how he felt, he replied with a touch of humility, "Me? I'm glad I'm alive."

From then on, Winchell was very careful when writing about gangsters.

Winchell himself described to a reporter a most embarrassing incident which occurred because of his associations with "the mob."

"One night I was in Dave's Blue Room talking to some of the boys when a fellow across the room crooked his finger at me and motioned for me to come over.

"I went over, and he said, out of the side of his mouth, 'Sit down there, you so-and-so, and keep your trap shut.' I think I sat down. Maybe I fell down. He was hopped up and he wasn't fooling.

"He sat down across the table from me and started to call me everything he could think of. All I could think of was what the boys had said about the way Rothstein was killed. Shot in the stomach under the table while he was talking to a guy. The mug kept saying, 'I'm going to kill you. Do you understand?' And all the blood drained out of my face and I was pretty sick.

"'Listen,' I said. 'I'm regular. Why, Owney Madden and me are just like that!'

"'Ta hell with Owney Madden,' said the killer, and the cold sweat popped out on me.

" 'Listen,' I said desperately. 'I know Frenchy too.' 'Ta hell with Frenchy,' says the guy.

" 'My God,' I said to myself. 'Who is this guy that talks about Owney and Frenchy like that?'

"IF ONLY SOMEBODY WOULD COME OVER HERE, I kept thinking, but I was afraid to look around or open my mouth. I can't tell you how long this lasted, but, after a while, a funny kind of a reaction set in. You can't go on being scared to death forever. Finally you get to the point where you say, 'Go ahead and get it over with.' I heard myself saying that, and got scared all over again, but some change seemed to come over this mug too.

" 'I'm going out of here the way I came in,' he said—which didn't mean anything to me, but sounded awful. And with that he got up and sort of oozed out the door. As soon as I could stand up without falling, I went out and told a cop to walk me home and not to tell anybody about it—which, of course he did.

"Several years later I was in Dave's Blue Room one night and a couple of the boys from the mob came over and said, 'Walter, there's a fellow here who wants to see you. He wants to apologize. He feels awful about something that happened once. He feels terrible.'

"It seems they were right. He wasn't a killer. He didn't belong to any mob. He was just a little toughy who had seen too many movies—and I guess I had seen too many, too, because he had sounded awful real to me."

But not even fear kept Winchell from making his appointed rounds of the night clubs in his early days. He went to all of them, alternately begging, then blustering, seeking "hot" stories, seeking "scoops."

He sat in smoke-filled rooms where people swallowed huge quantities of gut-rotting liquor, ate worse food, and danced to the collegiate moans of saxaphones.

Everything was served in the semi-darkness including the check. Had the food and drink been good, the guests wouldn't have known it. They were packed like rolled anchovies in a space about the size of an anchovy can.

Owney Madden and some of the others among the old-time mob went respectable. They retired on their "earnings" or invested them in legitimate businesses.

Winchell became lonely for the excitement of being with the toughies, or, as he called them, the "baddies."

By now he was also friendly with the Police Department of the City of New York. He had learned when to mention a name in his column.

He was on a first-name relationship with Bo Weinberg, "Dutch" Schultz, Joey Rao, "Big Bill" Dwyer and Arnold Rothstein. He became friendly with "Lucky" Luciano and the Fiaschetti brothers. But these friendships didn't interfere with his affections for the local police, or vice versa.

The police permitted him to tune in on police calls.

Now, when the saloons emptied at 3 a.m., he would romp about the darkened sleeping city in his car, which was equipped with a siren.

He would invite various people to join him in his early morning prowling.

For this hobby, he bought a Ford sedan because he read somewhere that gunman John Dillinger thought its pickup value was the best—especially for a fast getaway from the police.

Few of the people who joined him for a cops and robbers cruise ever asked for a repeat ride.

During the few years before his death that Damon Runyon associated with Winchell, Runyon called the automobile night prowling "kid stuff" and told friends he rode with his columnist companion only to watch the excitement on Winchell's face when an alarm came in.

Once the car sped to a holdup scene nearby, and arrived before the police car. Both Winchell and the holdup man were quite embarrassed. Winchell sat stiffly in the car, to the amusement of those with him. He waited for the police car to arrive. The holdup man had been so intrigued by the siren-equipped car from which nobody emerged that he'd just stood there, gun in hand, and also waited for the police.

After that, Winchell was never in so much of a hurry to arrive at the scene of a crime.

It was his press agent and part-time ghostwriter, Irving Hoffman, who received the tip that Lepke wanted to give himself up.

Lepke was wanted by both city and Federal authorities and had decided it would be safer to face the Federal charges. At that time Thomas E. Dewey was District Attorney of New York City and was out to build himself a record of convictions for political purposes.

Lepke selected Winchell because, as he later revealed, "I figured that if I was alone, some wise guy cop might put one in my belly, but I knew they wouldn't take a chance on the bad publicity that would come if they shot at me and killed Winchell."

Hoffman made the arrangements. Winchell met Lepke and the two men rode around for awhile chatting. Then, at the appointed time, Winchell drove to where they would meet J. Edgar Hoover.

The story didn't mean much to the papers. Even Winchell's own paper couldn't find room for it before page three. But to Winchell it was one of the most important things that had ever happened anywhere to anyone.

Years later, a book writer could be assured of plugs in Winchell's column by merely mentioning Winchell's bringing in Lepke. The book could be a Russian dictionary or a history of canned applesauce, but if the author would indicate with a paper clip the page where Winchell and Lepke are mentioned together, he could be assured of favorable publicity.

In later years, Winchell would meet J. Edgar Hoover during the trial of Bruno Hauptmann, the man convicted of kidnapping the Lindbergh baby. He developed a friendship with the FBI Director while maintaining his chummy relationship with the old-time mobsters.

Once when he visited Chicago, he was guarded by two cousins of Al Capone, the Fiaschetti brothers of recent Kefauver Committee fame. Two G-men were also part of his bodyguard at the same time . . . making for a unique and somewhat embarrassing situation for all.

To this day, Hoover assures all callers that despite what people believe, "Winchell has no pipeline to me or my office. He gets no information from me that isn't given to all other newspapermen at the same time."

Hoover's "friendship" with Winchell has caused Hoover occasional embarrassment.

There was a night at the Stork Club when J. Edgar Hoover, King of the G-Men, was playing with a toy machine gun while Walter Winchell, King of the Columnists, looked on approvingly. Photographers took pictures.

Terry Riley, a notorious gunman was also a Cub Room patron at the time.

Winchell didn't open his mouth when somebody suggested Hoover and Riley pose for pictures together.

Riley showed reluctance. He became ill at ease, the more so as Hoover in a jovial mood encouraged him.

It became obvious to Riley, as it must have been to Winchell, that Hoover didn't know who he was. He became more and more uncomfortable, refused to pose for the photographers and finally left the place.

Riley was on parole at the time for extortion and impersonating an FBI man.

One night while speeding around through the city streets with Mark Hellinger, Winchell complained that he never was able to get more than six hours sleep a day, mostly because of a nervous diarrhea.

"Why that's a lot of sleep," Hellinger replied. "That's plenty for you. Edison only got four hours sleep a night."

"Sure," mused Winchell in all seriousness, "but I need a clear mind. I've got important things to think about."

12

Bernarr Does a Burn

Bernarr Macfadden is a man in his late eighties, a spent Hercules in a packaged goods civilization. Carrots and spinach and celery can't be grown where the cement sidewalks lie on the street nineteen floors below him.

Instead the vegetables are grown in far away places with dangerous chemicals to protect them from insects, and other chemicals to make them grow faster and larger. They are boxed, canned, frozen or petrified—with more chemicals.

"Nothing is raw anymore," Macfadden complains, with his fading though still vibrant voice. "Nobody does any exercise anymore. Our people are becoming fat and flabby. They don't seem to remember the first principles of good health."

The people who were once physical culture addicts have gone on to bridge and canasta and scrabble. They sit at home evenings watching television, and who can do calisthenics in a television-darkened room.

But you can't down Bernarr Macfadden. When he isn't leaping from a plane with a parachute to demonstrate his good health, he is running for Mayor of New York to demonstrate his good citizenship.

It is typical of New York that it doesn't know Macfadden was running for Mayor. And it is typical of Macfadden that he doesn't care much.

He enjoys seeing a face (his) plastered on the front page of a one-shot tabloid (his) in which his fellow citizens are warned that there isn't much of anyone else around who could do as good a job.

His offices are in the *Daily News* building and from his private room which overlooks Forty-Second Street, he can stare across the street at the building which houses Macfadden Publications, a multi-million dollar magazine publishing and distribution business in which he no longer has a nickel's worth of interest.

"I've always been friendly with Winchell," he says. "I never had much to do with him. Oursler took care of those things."

Macfadden had once referred to the Winchell column as "a mass of unintelligible jargon."

Now he leaned toward the reporter.

"Gauvreau sold me out," he said. "We were negotiating to buy the *Mirror* from Hearst. It had already lost a couple of million. Then Gauvreau sold me out. He talked me into firing Winchell."

"I hear that Winchell helped," said the reporter. "I hear that he used to call you in the middle of the night and threaten to write that you were sneaking hamburgers and steak dinners into your diet while you claimed to be a vegetarian."

"I don't remember that," Macfadden said. He shook his head. "If Gauvreau hadn't sold me out we would have been the second paper in New York." He chuckled. "We were losing a lot of money. From the first day the *Graphic* began, we were losing five thousand dollars a day."

"That's a lot of money," the reporter said.

"It didn't matter," Macfadden explained. "We'd lose five thousand downtown at the *Graphic* and uptown the magazines were making ten thousand a day."

"What happened with Winchell," the reporter asked.

"You going to give him hell?" Macfadden grinned. "You're going to give Winchell hell?"

"Not exactly. I'm writing a book about him."

Macfadden chuckled again, and then he became solemn. "Gauvreau fixed it so that I'd fire Winchell. Winchell went to the *Mirror*. Then Gauvreau quit and went to the *Mirror*. We didn't have much chance after that at the *Graphic*."

"I know," the reporter said.

"If Gauvreau hadn't made me fire him, we would have been the second paper. Winchell was under contract for a long time more. *The Mirror* was going to be ours in a few months."

"Well, thanks," the reporter said.

"Good luck to you," Macfadden said. "I want to read that book. I hope I'll be around."

"I hope so," the reporter said.

Macfadden sighed and sat back in his reclining chair. He looked at the photographs on the wall. They were of himself and of the health resorts he used to run when he was a man with many millions of dollars and a determination to make humanity healthy with natural foods and good living.

He was an old man and could be forgiven if his memory wasn't in harmony with other versions of what happened.

Emile Gauvreau, the grandaddy of the American tabloid, remembers it differently.

Hearst had offered Winchell $500 a week to join his *Mirror*. $250 would be from the *Mirror* and $250 as a guarantee against syndicate royalties. Winchell, hungry for the additional money, decided to squirm out of his contract with the *Graphic* which still had some years to run.

"One forenoon Macfadden told me to discharge Winchell by releasing him from his contract. I fired him and he made a flying leap for the exit with a shout. I put Louis Sobel in his place and he soon caught on to Winchell's formula but he wrote in less heated vein."

The *Graphic* was to feed the roots of the worst personal feuds Winchell would know for many years.

Gauvreau was to become his bitterest hate. For a while too, he would feud with Louis Sobel who had replaced him.

But in the back pages of the *Graphic* was a sports columnist who would later make some of the frankest comments about his personal contempt for Winchell. His sports column was called Sport Whirl, and his name was Ed Sullivan.

13

The Mirror

Walter Winchell joined the *New York Daily Mirror* on June 10, 1929. He didn't appear in the Sunday edition of that paper until November 25, 1934.

The stock market crashed and Winchell tiptoed among its rubble, saying proudly, "Lucky for me, I didn't fall for any of those stocks I touted in the column." The market fell and Winchell rose.

On joining the *Mirror,* he resumed his column according to formula.

Hearst promotion men posted life-size cut-outs of him all over Manhattan. Winchell wanted them to go one better and put his name in lights around the top of the building.

The *Mirror* described him as "the keyhole connoisseur" and King Features Syndicate called him "the biggest and the best of the Broadway blab-boys."

Within a short time he could honestly boast that he had two hundred papers carrying his column.

"McIntyre only has a hundred eighty," he said dutifully, neglecting to mention that McIntyre's papers carried that column every day, while the Winchell column appeared in many papers only once or twice a week.

The *Commonweal,* a liberal weekly published by Catholic laymen noted on September 24, 1930 that:

"Editor & Publisher announces the interesting fact that a Mr. Walter Winchell, who, it seems, writes gossip

about Broadway celebrities, is paid $121,000 a year for his syndicate articles. A few years ago he was an inconspicuous vaudeville hoofer whose salary some weeks was $25."

Somebody at the *Commonweal* may have read the Winchell columns. They apparently didn't like what met the eye. Quoted the *Commonweal:* "There still remain a few things for which money is not the measure of value, and the winged words of truth are to be numbered among them."

Other critics were equally unkind.

J. P. McEvoy, who wrote several of the Ziegfeld Follies, said of Winchell in an article in the *Saturday Evening Post:* "Although you would suppose that Walter Winchell is settled, fixed, he betrays in a hundred ways the fear and the anxiety of the newcomer, of the *arriviste.* He is still sensitive about ridicule. He is taut and self-conscious of his role all the time.

"He cannot relax. He seems to be eternally vigilant, fearful of missing something. He seems to have no privacy, no retreat to which the human being Walter Winchell can sometimes find a shelter.

"He is constantly betraying a nervous, horrible fear of losing his punch, of being discarded as a vogue. He spends his vacations on Broadway. He has the dead pallor of the sunless.

"There is something pathetically infantile in the serious way in which he takes himself, in the intensity with which he pursues his little paragraphs of personalia."

But Winchell wasn't having any criticism.

He ignored critics until their criticism was no longer on sale at the neighborhood newsstands, and then he sunk his fangs into them with hint, innuendo and bold distortions of fact.

In later years, Broadwayites would talk about the "old Winchell" with some nostalgia. The "old Winchell" who combed the catacombs of spurious pleasure to report on the doings of celebrities and the sayings of the wise men of literature.

They watched him in his man battles. At times he seemed to be backed against the wall, single-handedly dueling a hundred men. At other times he seemed to be standing at the headstone of an enemy in the cemetery and beating the corpse to a second death.

Among those who knew him best, the belief is that from the beginning there was only one Winchell, the same Winchell who went to the *Mirror* in 1929. At no time did an "old" Winchell discard his shell for a "new" improved (or disintegrated) Winchell.

He has always been the same old spieler.

He has always used his column the way his gangster friends used their blackjacks or guns. The column was Winchell's gun, and where some guns had silencers, Winchell's column had none. Nor did it have scruples, decency or conscience.

The difference was that when Winchell used his column as a weapon of death, the sound of the shot didn't seem to repel his readers, whom he kept in a trance.

He would pop off his enemies one by one and the audience would say, "Isn't that column something though? How does he ever get away with it?"

The Broadway crowd who were later to become totally disenchanted with the columnist never had the foresight to recognize their own undoing in what he was doing to others.

"Winchell has blown his top," Irving Hoffman remarked in 1953. "I can't talk to him."

The truth is that Winchell never had a top. Or a bottom. There was no place to which he would not descend to hurt a foe. Every critic was a foe. And there was nothing sacred in his treatment of friends.

He was still the little boy from the East Side, hurling louder invectives at the gang than they could hurl at him. Slinging heavier filth.

"Did you see how I took care of him today?" he would

say with relish, upon "going after" someone who'd offended him.

His conscience was hidden under thick layers of callousness acquired since diaperhood.

His anger was ferocious. His malice unremitting.

If Mrs. J. Loose made repeated denials of the item: "Mrs. J. Loose, who has more money than her Loose-Wiles plants have biscuits, and Vice President Curtis are blazing . . . "—if she denied that they were more than acquaintances, Winchell replied, "Who says you're not blazing? I say you're blazing."

If Mrs. J. Loose persisted, Winchell would retaliate with an item like this:

A bisquit queen is very loose with her affections. She's lousy with dough, and I don't mean lard.

And then:

Friends would like to know why Mrs. J. Loose and Vice President Curtis have tiff'd?

When Winchell wrote on November 12, 1934: "Which Vanderbilt bachelor, there are five of them, has been secretly married a year?" he was wrong on two counts and one technicality.

There were not five Vanderbilt bachelors among "the" Vanderbilts. The Vanderbilt who'd been "married a year" had been married almost two. And if it was a "secret" to Winchell it was no secret to the readers of papers like the *New York Times* and *New York Herald-Tribune* where a full report of the marriage together with photographs had appeared.

The technicality is that the Vanderbilt who was married was no longer a bachelor.

When these matters were called to the attention of Winchell, his response was apt and revealing.

"Mr. Vanderbilt, others may have printed it, but I'm the guy who makes it public," he said, and walked away without waiting for a reply.

The people who fed items to Winchell found that an

easy way to get a column break was to tip him off to a birth, engagement, divorce or death.

His obituaries were often a little premature.

On November 5, 1935, under threat of a damage suit, he was forced to write:

Josephine Sexton is not dead, she says.

"If Winchell says you're dead, then you're better off dead for at least a year" became a newspapermen's cliché.

But the people he really wanted to die didn't always die as conveniently as he would have preferred.

Later, when he'd become a radio commentator, he made similar fluffs.

Captain Eddie Rickenbacker in the *American Magazine* in 1943 wrote: "Once I heard a voice on the radio beside my bed say, 'Flash! It is now confirmed that Eddie Rickenbacker is dying and will not live over an hour.'

"It was Walter Winchell. It made me madder than hell."

Rickenbacker betrayed Winchell by continuing to live at least another twenty years.

Winchell has never forgiven him.

14

An Early Feud

"He is no joke," wrote Alistair Cooke for the London Listener. "He is like some freak of climate—a tornado, say, or an electric storm that is heard whistling and roaring far away against which everybody braces himself: and then it strikes and does its whirling damage . . ."

In 1927 there were still some who asked, "Where did he come from? What is he like? Who, anyway, does he think he is?"

By 1930 those questions had been answered to the satisfaction of all who were seeking answers. He came from the East Side. He was like a dynamo. He thought he was the most important thing in American journalism, that his contribution of a gossip column was the greatest achievement of mankind since the first primitive man scratched the first words on the walls of a cave.

When he boasted that more people read him each morning than anyone else, it was no longer sheer loudmouthing. It was true.

When Arthur Brisbane said, "Winchell, you've got to grow. You have neither ethics, scruples, decency or conscience," the wonder boy replied, "Let others have those things. I've got the readers."

But circulation figures were never enough satisfaction. Nor was the increased income which had risen to a minimum of $1,000 a week.

The test was how "powerful" he was. How he could "kill 'em with one line in the column."

It was inevitable that he would make enemies. He turned on anyone where a tidbit was concerned.

Sime Silverman, one of the first persons to help and encourage him, became a Winchell victim.

Silverman, editor of *Variety*, married, was then carrying on an affair with Renee Davies. All three of the Davies sisters were mistresses of prominent publishers, with sister Marion catching the biggest fish in William R. Hearst.

Now, Silverman's wife was aware of her husband's fluctuating fidelity. Like many wives, she kept her sorrow to herself and hoped that the flirtation would be done with quickly.

Winchell published a blind item about the affair, using initials so that all could be certain who the "show biz trade publisher" was.

On the fifth floor of the *Variety* office was a room with a couch where Silverman occasionally lived with the Davies woman. As a gag, Jimmy Durante had a small neon sign set outside the fifth floor door which read "Chateau De Layem."

Winchell carried this too.

Silverman complained to Damon Runyon: "I don't mind his ingratitude. I enjoyed seeing him get started. But apart from any personal considerations, isn't there a vein of decency in him?"

Silverman had only one conversation with Winchell, on the street, before he barred him from the *Variety* offices and stopped talking to him.

"Winchell, you've got a girl friend now, haven't you? How do you think Hattie felt when she read that drivel in your column?"

"I didn't mean you, Sime—" Winchell started to alibi, backing away.

"How would June like it if I ran an item on the front page of *Variety* advertising your extra-marital affair?"

Winchell tried to muster a grin. "You go ahead, Sime. You do that. She knows the score anyway."

Silverman turned his back on Winchell and walked away in disgust.

A prominent comedian poured a pitcher of ice-water over Winchell's head in Lindy's restaurant. "You're so hot about my personal life," he explained, "I thought this would be a good way to cool you off."

"I'll get you for that," Winchell muttered.

In this particular case, the way he "got" the comedian was never to mention him again.

Despite the wilful damage he was wreaking on many lives, Winchell actually trembled with rage and fear when his column was criticized. Criticism brought on a reflex. It would cause him to arch his back, sharpen his claws and strike back in the column.

Mark Hellinger too was coming into his own on Broadway. Both Hellinger and Winchell commanded respect from some because of the wide readership each wrote for.

Winchell copied Hellinger's dressing habits. Soon both men were wearing nothing but dark blue suits with navy blue shirts and bright yellow ties.

In that way were they alike. They were different in many ways. For instance Hellinger could never allow anyone else to reach for a restaurant check, while it is said that if Winchell ever reached for a check, the new form of exercise would break his arm, to say nothing of how it would break his heart.

Hellinger was lavish with tips, often handing the hat check girl, headwaiter, waiter, busboy and men's room attendant a couple of dollars each, though his meal check might be ninety-five cents.

Winchell was and is to this day a ten-cent tipper.

On a warm night in February, 1932, a number of Broadway people were guests at a midnight dinner given by Sidney Solomon. Solomon was a restaurant owner who had become "one of the boys" because of his friendship with Mayor Jimmy Walker.

During the dinner, guest of honor Earl Carroll was called upon to say a few words. What he said was most unexpected.

He rose from his seat and faced Winchell. "Walter Winchell," he declared, "you are not fit to associate with decent people. You give it to a lot of others, now let's see if you can take some of it yourself."

The vaudevillian in Winchell forced him to say: "That's O.K. with me, Earl."

Carroll shook his head sadly at the corny response and walked to the back of the Casino where he wept.

This incident in Winchell's social history might have ended there among the embarrassed diners had not restaurateur Solomon stood up.

In a loud voice he told the guests that he agreed thoroughly with the sentiments of Earl Carroll. Then he turned on Mark Hellinger. "You're just another flashy bum like your friend Winchell over there. Everything I said about him goes for you too."

Hellinger was not one to be trifled with in such an unseemly manner. His fists doubled impulsively as he blurted to a lady companion: "Watch me sock that bird just once to maintain my self-respect."

Winchell overheard the threat. He called, "Say, Mark, when did you develop self-respect?"

The next day, both columnists wrote their separate versions of the affair. Each man labeled his own story a "scoop."

The incident attracted the attention of Marlen Pew, the editor of *Editor & Publisher*.

He wrote of the columnists in his back page editorial: "These are the creators of the 'new culture' which circles about the Broadway column, babbles an audacious brand of illiteracy, sets up a new concept of decency in human relations and has as its bugle call the Bronx razz."

Hellinger thought Pew's remarks were "cute" but Winchell couldn't take it. He had been constantly criticized by Pew for his irresponsibility in not checking easilycheckable stories. He had referred to Pew as "Marlen Pee-yew."

Pew wrote further that: "I hear that Broadway columnists hold regular meetings in midtown hotels nowadays to discuss various topics of their trade.

"Inevitably this will lead to the writing of a code of ethics. What an interesting document it would be! I dare say they will tell us just what 'news' is. Evidently American journalism has long had a very limited view of the possibilities of what may and what may not be said in print. No doubt the new code will make it clear why a guess is as good as an authenticated fact in news columns.

"And too, we may learn just how far a reporter may peek behind the curtains of private lives. At some early meeting the boys might take up the grave implications in a line of type which recently appears in Winchell's column, as follows: 'The best known film magnate attempted suicide last week.'

"Was that nice? There are so many 'best known film magnates,' each with a wife, children and friends, that such anonymous publications might conceivably work much wrong and give considerable pain.

"The suggestion is offered that the item contained no truth but was one of those spontaneous hunches that may easily pour from an undisciplined brain onto a permanent printing surface when stirring copy is feverishly needed and nobody is reading manuscript."

Pew concluded: "I have no stomach for the job of regulating the journalistic morals of the white light paragraphers, being perfectly willing to let Broadway sewage find its own way to the sea."

This was fair comment from a highly honored man in American journalism.

Winchell's response was typical of the pattern he would eventually set for himself in dealing with all critics.

In a column headed "Portrait of A Man Talking To Himself" he wrote:

Well, I've always been lucky that way . . . I mean about sharp-shooters who make me their target . . . I knew that if my patience held out that eventually things would even themselves, and now I haven't the heart to let both barrels go . . . He has been making speeches at schools of journalism and at various colleges denouncing tabloid papers—usually singling me out for a piece of his alleged mind, and because he represents a distinguished newspaper trade magazine, of course, he must have been believed . . . He blames me for the "Front Page" show and movie, which he asserts 'libels' the craft . . . He has called me everything from 'a journalistic gangster' to names I've forgotten . . .

Now, I can take plenty of slugging, but I discovered that he himself is a 'reformed' disgracer of the newspaper profession he says I disgrace . . . He was once arrested for criminal libel when he edited a "yellow" and sensational Philadelphia rag . . . His vicious abuse, animosity and virulence against the late Calvin Coolidge, in 1924, were ignored by Cal with his characteristic bigness, but Party leaders and George B. Lockwood, who edited the National Republican, decided not to let him get away with his attacks—and they exposed his arrest for criminal libel in the National Republican . . . That was in the April 12, 1924, issue of that journal . . . The story in that issue adds that police authorities decided not to press the charges provided he left town . . . And the charges had not been dismissed . . . Yet, this finger-pointer has the gall to appoint himself as my severest critic . . .

Yes, it took me almost 5 years to get weary of 'taking it'—5 years, perhaps, of 'justified' scoldings, without my whimpering once! . . . Because, of course, it took me 5 years to get hep to him! . . . I prefer not to mention the name of the magazine he now pilots because it is respected by us all, but I cannot refrain from reminding the craft that a man, who was fired by such distinguished organizations as the Munsey, Scripps and Hearst newspapers, and who was arrested for criminal libel—is hardly qualified to appoint himself as dictator of American journalistic ethics . . . And I withhold his name from the public—only to give him a lesson in newspaper ethics—which he alleges I abuse.

On January 14, 1933, Marlen Pew lowered the boom on Walter Winchell. "A great many people have suffered injury and indignity at the hands of Walter Winchell," he began, "but few have stepped forth to call his bluffs.

"He is considered by some an American untouchable. To sue him is to touch pitch. So, the Broadway scavenger has enjoyed remarkable immunity and seems to feel unusual power. This confidence does not extend beyond his barricade, however. He is a physical coward. I would estimate that not one libel suit is brought per thousand libels committed in his column during the past five years. The nearest he has come to the danger line was when a New York grand jury took notice of the fact that he had predicted a racketeer 'spot murder' in this city some months ago. He apparently had advance information. Among racketeers he is a hero. Respectable people flee from such menaces as Winchell and not without reason. Better to ignore his libels than wallow. In one respect this is sensible, because Winchell is now so thoroughly revealed, thanks to a few courageous playwrights, magazine writers, columnists and others, that the public must discount his daily blather almost entirely. You know, of course, that the comedy and movie 'Blessed Event,' were fairly accurate descriptions of the Winchell business. Not all of it, nor the worst part of it, but enough to convince the reading public that 'news' from that source may be disregarded.

"Winchellism comes within the purview of *Editor & Publisher*. We have not hesitated to attack it as menacing the good name of journalism. Inevitably, the journalistic gangster would put me 'on the spot.' Today, I see in his column, which is syndicated by King Features and published locally in the *Mirror*, he libels me without using my name, or the name of this journal.

"I could sue him and doubtless make it stick, as I could have sued George B. Lockwood, editor of the erstwhile *National Republican*, a weekly that used to be sold in bundle lots to beneficiaries of the tariff and other forms of privilege, when he originated 8 years ago the libels Winchell has now picked up. Lockwood induced a newspaperman, whom I had previously, as a Hearst executive, discharged for disloyal conduct, to write me up in his *National Republican*, the object being to intimidate me, as I was then criticizing Republican press agents for stuff they were handing out on the Teapot Dome oil scandal. The name of Calvin Coolidge was never mentioned in those articles, and I had reason to believe the President had no knowledge of the palpably deceitful party press releases.

"Though the provocation was great, and the offense described by a New York legal expert as 'libel per se,' I did not sue Lockwood, but so great was the alarm among cabinet-member sponsors of the *National Republican* that they presently withdrew their names and Lockwood was compelled to accept responsibility for the paper without the support of distinguished party leaders. Nor do I propose to sue Winchell. Probably I can protect myself by my own means amd my hide has thickened during the jazz age.

"Lest some reader of this journal be misled, to my detriment, it is perhaps advisable that I set forth here an answer to Winchell's published statements of Jan. 11. First, he complains because I call him a 'journalistic gangster.' I'll give a red apple to anyone who can write a better description of his work. In his article, Winchell charges: 'He was once arrested for criminal libel when he edited a 'yellow' and sensational Philadelphia rag.'

"I edited the Scripps newspaper *News-Post,* in Philadelphia, for two years, and count it the best experience of my life. I was arrested for criminal libel, and put in a cell incommunicado, at midnight, and later held in the highest cash bail ever known in that city for such a charge. The complainant was a Penrose-McNichol political gangster, Jimmy Carey, Fifth Ward political tyrant, and member of the minor judiciary of that gang-ridden city. I had published the affidavit of a park policeman, Independence Square by the way, that Carey had offered him a $25 bribe, while he was sitting as a juryman in the equity case of a poor man and his wife, to swing the verdict in favor of a local traction company.

"I never could get my libel case tried, though I repeated the charge time and again, and nearly every day demanded editorially that the District Attorney bring

the case before a jury. So far as I know the indictment is
still pigeonholed, covered by the dust of 20 years. My
partners in that newspaper venture were the late E. W.
Scripps, Roy W. Howard, and the late Hamilton Clark.
Depend upon it, the jury-bribing case was never tried,
but one of the last official acts of Senator Boies Pen-
rose was to elevate Carey on the public payroll. Winchell
would not understand that sort of newspaper work. The
best he could get out of it is that I was 'arrested,' the dis-
creditable implication being left obscure.

"It was something to rattle in the column. It is typical
of his malice. He probably never heard that in Philadelphia the late Charles Emory Smith and the late E. A. Van
Valkenburg, really famous editors who had fought the
same battle I took a fling at, were so often arrested for
'criminal libel' that it became a national joke. They, also,
were unable to get their cases before a jury.

"Winchell writes: 'His vicious abuse, animosity and
virulence against the late Calvin Coolidge, in 1924, were
ignored by Cal with characteristic bigness, but party
leaders and George B. Lockwood, who edited the *National Republican,* decided not to let him get away with
his attacks—and they exposed his arrest in the *National
Republican.* . . . The story in that issue adds that the
police authorities decided not to press the charges provided he left town.'

"That's the way Winchell writes 'news.' It is the perfect flower of the journalistic mobster on the job. I have
noted the facts. My departure from Philadelphia had
nothing to do with the libel case, which was then a dead-
letter. Roy Howard knows the story. He and Mr. Scripps
asked me at that time to remain with the Scripps organization, in a much higher capacity, but I had plans of my
own. I was fairly paid, my resignation is a matter of
record and they remained my faithful friends.

"Says Winchell: "I cannot refrain from reminding the
craft that a man, who was fired by such distinguished
organizations as the Munsey, Scripps and Hearst news-

papers, and who was arrested for criminal libel—is hardly qualified to appoint himself as dictator of American journalistic ethics.'

"Leave it to Winchell to take up the dictatorship and prescribe ethics! Mr. Munsey is dead, but I guess Bob Davis and Keats Speed would remember that I never worked for a Munsey newspaper. I worked for Scripps three times, and one of the last things the Old Man ever said to me was that I was an 'unfrocked priest' out of his organization, and suggested I rejoin him. His organization, however, seems to have prospered without my ministrations. I was never discharged from the Scripps service.

"The Appellate Division of the Supreme Court of New York is authority for the fact that I was not discharged by the Hearst service. I thought that Moses Koenigsberg, in 1922 in charge of the Hearst services and syndicates, had fired me, without justification and breaching a Hearst contract, but the court said 'No.' Koenigsberg sent my salary for many weeks after, as a matter of principle, I had walked out of his office.

"I sent back the checks. A jury in the State Supreme Court heard the story, and gave me a verdict which represented the exact amount of the unexpired contract, on the theory that I had been discharged. The higher court upset this, on the theory that I had not. Later a jury decided I had not been discharged. Only Winchell and I think to the contrary. It would be worth $50,000 to me if I could prove it.

"All of which, being personal discussion, is rather embarrassing, but this is my forum and while it isn't very terrible to be fired, or arrested or mobbed in honest newspaper endeavor, I wish to be understood by my readers. I have more interesting things to write about in this space but some good will come of this week's instalment, aside from personal allusions, if editors of the land get a better view of the real meaning of Winchellism."

Shortly thereafter Winchell suffered his second "nervous breakdown." The first had followed the time gangsters had threatened to cast him in cement.

The Pew feud had a many-fold effect on the life and times of Walter Winchell.

For one thing, it made clear to the journalistic fraternity something Winchell already knew: that he had never established any real working relationship with the working press.

Also that he was not respected by most of his fellow newspapermen.

Finally and most important, that in any fight he would allow no scruples or ethics to deter him from smearing the enemy. Nor would he give truth a sideways glance.

Winchell has invariably succeeded in his back biting when the enemy of the moment had no means of replying.

If Winchell wrote: "John Jones, who has criticized this column was arrested in 1932 and 1934. Pleaded guilty in both instances. This is a matter of police record. Judge Koch did the sentencing," he was reaching some eleven million people, some of whom probably knew John Jones.

It would be difficult enough for Jones to tell his friends, let alone the other part of the eleven million that his so-called arrests were for speeding, and that the "sentences" were $1 and $2 fines respectively.

But Winchell was at a disadvantage with Marlen Pew. He couldn't name Pew, even in his rage, for that would have been stepping too squarely on the hot coals of libel.

The only people who recognized whom he meant were newspapermen. And they read Pew's side of the story. And understood.

Pew was a legendary hero among newspapermen. Winchell was an upstart. And the hero had revealed the upstart to be a malicious liar.

It was the first, but not the last time that Winchell was to be cut down to pigmy size in front of the very people whose admiration he needed and craved.

15

The Next Voice You Hear

George Washington Hill, President of the American Tobacco Company, liked his music with a beat. When his Lucky Strike dance program was being broadcast, he would plug in a radio at an empty studio three floors above the broadcast studio. Then, with a broomstick as his only companion, he would dance about the studio with a tremendous vigor, jumping and bouncing and leaping in time to the rhythm. When the program was over he would fall, bathed in his own perspiration and with happy exhaustion, to the carpeted floor.

Lucky Strike cigarette commercials were comparatively short then. They consisted of a few lines about "Luckies are toasted. And being toasted they are your throat protection—against irritation—against cough . . ."

In 1931 it was decided by his physician that George Washington Hill must take a break or two during his program so that his heart wouldn't be subject to the continuous strain of dancing around in the empty studio.

Hill had been a Winchell reader. It was Hill who suggested that Winchell be given five minutes on the Lucky Strike program.

"They like his gossip in the papers, right?" he told his advertising agency. "Maybe they'll like to listen to it, right?"

"Right!" responded the agency.

So it was that Winchell was offered to America's ears as well as its eyes.

For five minutes every Saturday night, he held the attention of millions of Americans with his machine-gun delivery. He gobbled at his listeners at the rate of 127 words a minute.

"Do you know why I talk so fast?" he asked. "If I talked slowly, people would find out what I was saying and remember how dull it was."

He bounced up and down in his armchair and yelled secrets at a tremendous audience. He was correct in believing that not everybody could understand 127 words a minute. But it all sounded very important and very exciting.

When he saw his salary rise to $550 for each week's 1,635 words, he knew he had found a mecca.

"How long has this been going on?" he asked, when he showed his check to a group of bookies gathered in Lindy's Restaurant.

"What was that stuff you were saying about Syria?" one of the men at the table asked.

"What's Syria?" Winchell grinned.

Suddenly the conversation became menacingly quiet.

"What's wrong? What did I say?"

"I'm Syrian," the man said. "I don't like people joking about Syria."

"Gee, I'm sorry," Winchell said. "I'll tell you what. I'll get a script in the morning and look at it. I can't ever remember a damned thing after the broadcast. You know me."

"I know you," the man said. "You be careful what you say about Syria."

Winchell slunk away.

Later, Winchell found proprietor Leo Lindeman. "Can you imagine that loud mouthed son of a bitch," Winchell said. "Doesn't he know about free speech?"

"Walter, you worry about your free speech, let me worry for my pastrami. But no fights. You fight in here and you never come in again."

Hear the voice of the prophet: "Adolph and Benito have phffft. The break will be officially announced soon enough."

Hear the geography teacher: "Fares on the London to Paris trains will be reduced in April."

Hundreds of listeners by telegraph, telephone and letter pointed out that London and Paris were separated by a body of water called the English Channel.

Winchell didn't stop talking long enough to listen.

"Next to aspirin and hangover remedies," said Winchell, "Winchell is the leading stimulant for Broadway, Hollywood and Park Avenue."

"Winchell talks about himself as though he has just left the table," said sportswriter Jimmy Cannon.

"It is possible," wrote Harry Salpeter in "The Outlook," "that for some part of the day, Walter Winchell lives his own, his private life. The burden of proof is to the contrary. Walter Winchell is not preeminently a man. Walter Winchell is a quality."

Never shy, never modest, Winchell reprinted the statement to hand out to friends who invited him to their homes.

"Winchell doesn't go to homes," said Winchell.

The five minute broadcasts were sloppy in the beginning. But they provided the rest period for the man with the broomstick in the studio upstairs.

"Did you hear this fellow Winchell?" people were saying. "Boy does he talk fast."

"What does he say?" people were asking.

"I don't know. But it was highly confidential and very secret. He said so himself."

"Wow."

Later, on the night of March 29, 1937, he would premiere on radio with his own chatter program, sponsored by Jergens. Every Sunday night at nine, people would stop doing what they were doing to hear what he was saying.

"Hello Mr. and Mrs. America and all the ships at sea, let's go to press."

The familiar staccato voice, heralding twelve and one-half minutes of the Jergens Journal. Twelve and one-half minutes about who was sleeping with whom, about whom *who* wasn't going to sleep with anymore, and about the anticipated result of any healthy sperm making whoopie with any healthy ovum.

"Dots and dashes with lots of flashes from border to border and coast to coast . . ."

Tapping a telegraph key wildly, though he never bothered to learn the Morse code. Ripping at his necktie. Nuzzling against the microphone. Filling his hatband with nervous sweat. Gobbling at twenty-million pairs of ears.

"What famous movie actress isn't going to like this one . . ."

"Omigahd!"

"Ho hum . . ."

"Heheheh!"

"Looka whooz talkin!"

"Fervensakes!"

"Izzatso?"

"And that, Mr. and Mrs. America, winds up another Winchell, until next Sunday night. Until then, and with lotions of love, this is your favorite newsboy Walter telling you to take good care of yourself, because if you don't, ain't nobody else who will! Goodnight now!"

After studying a photograph of Walter Winchell's nervous fox-like face, examining a column, and hearing his breathless voice on the radio, a psychiatrist classed Winchell as suffering from "sublimated voyeurism."

"He is," said the psychiatrist, "a man who passionately

wants to see, to know, hating a secret, vicariously participating in all the things he sees and learns about and living everybody's life."

Herbert Marshall McLuhan in his folklore of industrial man titled "The Mechanical Bride" gave his impressions of a Winchell broadcast in four sentences:

Mr. and Mrs. North America, get a load of my tommy-gun rattle, rat-a-tat-tattle.

Wrap me in the flag after the battle and bury me under the prairie?

Look, Mom, I'm . . . Is there anybody alive in the audience?

Let's go to the cleaners?

16

The Hecklers

The voice of prophesy was on the land.

"You would no more sound the Winchell column for truth than you would an absorbing fairy story," wrote a critic.

They heckled him from everywhere but it was often in fun.

The magazine *College Humor* quipped that "People who live in glass houses shouldn't live next door to Walter Winchell."

To which Winchell replied: "Oh come now. People who live in glass houses can think up a better one than that."

Someone punched him. He insisted it wasn't a current girl friend at all but a Nazi. Sensing news value, he announced the fact to the reporters who called.

"There were two of them," he said. "They spoke German. They may have cost me a tooth."

The *Herald-Tribune* gave it four paragraphs. All of which caused Heywood Broun to write in *The Nation:*

"I'm quite ready to admit that if Walter Winchell is punched, that is news, although I would not put it in the list of either epochal or strange incidents.

"Mr. Winchell's tooth broke for the evening papers. Moreover, I had seen him before the *Herald Tribune* story appeared, and he assured me that no tooth had been knocked out. The *cause celebre* boiled down to the fact that a pivot tooth had been slightly loosened. It was already wired back into place by the time Mr. Reid's newsboys were disseminating the momentous and slightly distorted material."

Complaining that Winchell's loose tooth had received more newspaper notice in the *Herald-Tribune* than a local union convention (which received no mention) Broun went on to concede: "I do not know that the works of Walter Winchell may not all be printed on vellum immediately after his death and preserved for posterity."

In the *Mirror*, Winchell had sprung from the amusement section to page ten, where he remained.

When asked how he got his news, he would glibly avoid a direct answer by saying: "I get my stuff from a lot of people who promised somebody they would keep it a secret."

Actually, he had begun to depend almost exclusively on press agents for his material.

One column which he sometimes wrote himself was headed: "Portrait of A Columnist Talking to Himself."

Brevities ran a burlesque on this one with a column titled "Portrait of a Columnist Thinking to Himself."

It began with an introduction explaining that the idea of Winchell thinking to himself "is quite absurd and impossible; therefore no apologies for the following drivel should be necessary."

The burlesque began:

Gee, it would be great to be able to write just what I really think about to myself. . . . Wouldn't it burn some people up! . . . In this racket you have to be polite to so many people . . . just because they give you gags . . . when you'd really like to spit in their collective eye. . . . It's tough. . . . Still, some guys get away with it. . . . Take Sobol, for instance. . . . I'll bet if you were to punch him on that beak of his, he'd never get sore. . . . He'd just come back with: . . . "O. K., ol' pal, Whaddye know for Friday?" . . . S'funny, though. . . . Maybe Jimmie Durante was right—"It's a livin'." That's a swell line. . . . .

Take the troubles I've got, though. . . . That guy
Schmooze, for example. . . . Here I've been giving
him regular plugs for himself and his shows . . . for
months and months. . . . And for What! . . . just 40
lousy items a week and a couple of moth-eaten gags
that he copies out of Wehman Bros.' joke books. . . .
And now he turns over to the enemy and hands that
palookah Sullivan all his stuff. . . . That's gratitude
for you. . . . But it's Broadway just the same. . . .
Dear old Broadway, with its back-stabbers and
phoneys. . . . Hmmmm . . . I wonder if McIntyre
makes more than I do. . . . S'funny how he can write
his stint a month ahead and they still buy it, even if
he never had the sense to bribe an obstetrician's assistant . . . I wonder (nope, I shouldn't have said that,
Sullivan uses it all the time) . . . I'd like to know just
how many people read Mark's stuff . . . I think it's
pretty swell . . . but I constantly come across fellows
that say they can't read it. . . . It's too solid. . . .
They like short, snappy paragraphs that don't disturb
the fat behind the ears. . . .

My, my, my, it's getting late. . . . I'll have to knock
together the rest of that column if I'm going to meet
Gertie from Cracow over at the Blue Ointment Room.
. . . Let's see, what do I have to write about. . . . Gee!
It's that sob column on how much I miss the wife and
kiddies . . . and how they tug at my heart strings
even when I'm mugging some blonde in the back room
of the Club Jason. . . . That's Broadway, too! . . .
Just a pack of lies and Bright Lights. . . . Oh, yes, and
broken hearts. . . . Those sob columns bring in a pack
of mail, though. . . . I don't know why. . . . They're
as easy to do as blowing your nose. . . .

Aha! Here's an advance copy of "Variety." . . .
Wow! That's a swell crack they have on the front page
box . . . just what I'm looking for. . . . Hmmmm.

. . . Lemme think. . . . Woops, I have it! . . . I'll lift it and credit it to a phoney correspondent from San Bernardino, California. . . . Then, that'll give me the prior claim to it. . . . It takes five days for the mail to come from the Coast . . . . Clever, eh, wot? . . . Here's a funny thing . . . I prophesied a blessed event for Mrs. Athanasius Piltz . . . and it didn't pan out. . . . I wouldn't be surprised if she went and had an illegal operation just to spite me. . . . You never can tell what some people will do just to inconvenience others. . . . And they just named a baloney sandwich after me in Reuben's . . . Mmmmm! . . . I wonder if that's a rib? . . . Too bad about that gag about the Empire State Tower and Al Smith. . . . I've tried my best, but I can't clean it up. . . . Well, life is full of disappointments. . . .

That's too bad about Sam, who runs the Beeway chatter column for The Unkblot. . . . He has no sense of humor at all . . . and he can't stand kidding, so he makes a fool of himself regularly . . . but if he ever mentions my name in that column of his again, I'll get him smacked. . . . S'help me!

Still, look at Joe, my best pal. . . . Gahd, what I wouldn't do for that guy! . . . He's one of the fairest, squarest, cleanest men on or near the Main Stem. . . . Yet he ran one of my gags in his column only yesterday, and never gave me credit. . . . The Rat! . . . That's Broadway friendship and generosity for you. . . .

Paul Zilch, one of my best contribs, also gives items to Gus Glomp. . . . I have a sneaky feeling that he gives Gus the best items . . . but I can't tell for sure. . . . Still, I get a chill whenever I see Gus grab the check when they're out together. . . . I wonder if this new star reporter they just took on will chisel in on my stuff. . . . He's edging too near Broadway for my comfort . . . Still, he don't know the ropes. . . . And I won't break a leg introducing him around. . . . There's too many damn stars on this paper already!

Howinell can I get around that "Must" reviews of the Dew Drop Inn. . . . The mob is expecting me to rave over it . . . but Heaven knows the most knock-kneed women in New York have been picked for their chorus . . . and that Master of Ceremonies! . . . He makes Jean Malin look like Bull Montana. . . . If they gave my little whoopie-partner Lulu a part, I might be able to uncork a few adjectives . . . But, again, I gotta be careful. . . . Mustn't mention girl-friends' names too often . . . the gang gets wise. . . . They've already accused me of having affairs with everybody from Mrs. Fiske to Baby Paggy on account of raves. . . .

Well, I'm getting down to the bottom of the page. . . . Wotta snap! Wotta snap! . . . I wish I could write one of these rambling columns every day instead of once a week. . . . They're better than air for filling space. . . . And you get paid for it, too. . . . Wotta Snap!

Others did satirical takeoffs on the column. H. I. Phillips did one in *The Evening Sun* which Winchell liked.

He was not quite so fond of the columns done by Ed Sullivan and Westbrook Pegler.

Wrote Pegler in a very apt parody of the Winchell column:

"I must remember to write something nice about George Washington. He deserves it, even from me. Walnuts grow on trees. Shakespeare died at the age of fifty . . .

"I wonder if its true. I mean about what I mean. I mean about the rumor of what I mean. It certainly will prove what I mean if I mean what I mean . . .

"I must remember to put that blast on Pontius Pilate . . ."

17

Stereopticon

See him as they saw him then. See Walter Winchell in the Broadway-Hollywood night club arena.

A column, at least once a week, in two hundred newspapers. A five minute newscast on Saturday night. A daily column in the *Daily Mirror*.

The year of breadlines was passing. Farmers in the midwest were still talking revolution, but that too would pass.

As the new Roosevelt Administration took over the reins of leadership, the leading rumor-seller was Winchell. He was an extension of what was happening all over the nation—people were dealing in rumors. Rumors would sweep from San Francisco to Presque Isle, Maine, in a matter of a week or two.

Winchell cut the time.

Rumors and the sayings and doings of the stars were enough to satisfy the whims of the people out front—for awhile.

He had paid off his loans from the Morris Plan banks. He was keeping a wife, two daughters, a mistress, and a $700 Ford sedan, and he had accumulated a large fortune.

Along with many other newspaper employees, he heard in advance that the banks were all going to close in the early days of Mr. Roosevelt's first administration.

Soon afterward, the following story was making the rounds:

It seems that Winchell had his money in many banks. And when he got the tip about the bank closings, he appeared practically simultaneously at all "his" banks requesting his money.

And, so the story goes, all the bankers were very reluctant. This made Winchell more anxious.

One banker was friendlier than the others. He greeted Winchell with open arms, a pat on the back, and an item for the column about the bank janitor and the chambermaid in the next apartment house.

The banker said, "Sure Walter, take your money. Take all of it. We're always willing to be of service to Walter Winchell. You know that."

This, so the story goes, impressed Winchell. He felt a little embarrassed about having doubted such a decent fellow. So he took all his money he had withdrawn from the other banks and put it into this nice fellow's nice bank.

And, so the story goes, all the banks closed on schedule —and they all opened up again. Except the bank in which Walter had banked all his money. That one never opened up again. And never will.

When J. P. McEvoy questioned Winchell about the incident, Winchell assured him it was all a fable.

"A good story," Winchell said to McEvoy, "but it isn't so. I never lost a penny in my life. I've never owned a stock. I've never invested in any business."

Winchell then proceeded to explain what "really" happened.

It seems that he had received the tip about the banks closing, all right. So he went to one bank he didn't trust where he had all his money.

"I want my money," he said. "I'm Walter Winchell."

It seems, according to Winchell that "They counted out half a million dollars in one-dollar bills and I carried it across the street to another bank in my arms—just like that!"

"Add Things You Never Knew Till Now, Mr. Winchell," wrote McEvoy when reporting the incident. "A package of one hundred new one-dollar bills weighs three and one-quarter ounces. Five thousand of these packages or $500,000 weighs 1,015 pounds and 10 ounces."

Amen.

See him as they saw him then.

J. P. McEvoy describes him as "Broadway's magpie flying home to his nest with every glittering trifle he can capture."

"This," says McEvoy, in an article for *Saturday Evening Post* titled "He Snoops to Conquer," "—this, is Mrs. Winchell's boy Walter, who never grew up—still playing cops and robbers. This is little Boy Peep blowing his horn with a vengeance."

See him as they saw him then.

He has become a man about town. He is so proud of his current mistress that he takes her everywhere, pawing her in public, kissing her cheeks, her fingers.

The embarrassment is so great to June Winchell that she locks him out of their apartment. He rents a suite in a hotel room and cuts off her income.

"Do you want your daughters to starve?" she says.

They reconcile and he promises to "reform."

But night clubs are no reform school. And his ego needs the constant soothing fingers of a new flame, a new woman to show off as his.

He reports his battles with his wife in the column. This gives him an opportunity too to boast of new conquests.

"Lay late," he writes, "and began the day with a quarrel with my sugar whose door I didn't mean to slam as I departed. It seems I am luckier in the dice house than I am in hers."

And two days later:

"In the hay till noon again, and hastened to keep a rendezvous with Eula Youngblood, as lovely a cowgirl as Oklahoma ever bred."

Or again in the column:

"Visited Vivian and Pearl at the Commodore, and the house detective was reluctant to permit me to remain, but fell for my police card. . . ."

And again:

"Helen Plunkett, shaplier than ever, and attired in attractive garments, was a sight for my eyes. So I took her to Schraffts . . . Later with Miriam Dolt who left her husband because he would not permit her to return to the stage. I comforted her as best I knew how. . . ."

One day readers are treated to a confession:

"I am disgusted with myself for living such an existence," he writes, "and pledged to cavort less hereafter, but Lord, I fear I will not be able to control my will, having had girl trouble since my 16th year."

At this point, June Winchell tells him she will never be seen with him in public.

"Do you want them to laugh at me? I'm your wife, not just another of your tarts."

"I can't help it," he mutters.

"That's all right. That's you. But I'm me. I'll keep house for you and bring up your daughters. But don't expect me to make a spectacle of myself by appearing with you."

True to her word, she never again made a public appearance with him, never attended a theater opening, never went to a night club with him.

See him as they saw him then.

His manner has about it the atmosphere of a dynamo, out of control, running in double-time, drunk on the ether of perpetual motion.

"Listen kid, stick with me and I'll make you a millionaire," he promises Irving Hoffman.

"That's not my cup of tea," Hoffman replies.

"That's a good line," says Winchell, pulling out pad and pencil. "Don't say anything else till I jot it down."

Hoffman shows him how to make words percolate with puns. He uses "microphony" to describe Rudy Vallee; "America's Swedeheart" for Greta Garbo.

Hoffman is slow-moving, thoughtful, slow-talking. He watches the dynamo spin around him. Swisshhh. Swisssshhh. Bloop. Blop. Bleep. "Listen Walter," he says, "now that you're working for Hearst, why don't you have them print your column in red ink?"

"I'll think about it," Winchell says, racing off to another night spot.

But the next morning he approaches publisher Arthur Brisbane to ask if the red ink is possible.

Brisbane suggests that he use boldface type and so the next Monday column appears in alternating light and bold, making it even more breathless, more startling, more intimate.

A few days later, Brisbane complains to his editor: "Can you imagine that fathead Winchell? He hustled into my office today and wanted me to read clippings about him. Does he think *we're* working for *him?*"

See him as they saw him then.

Broadway Brevities which labels itself "America's First Tabloid Weekly" carries an item which says: "If Walter Winchell and Louis Sobol don't stop that school-boy arguing, a few of the boys with white coats will call and take them places . . ."

Winchell steals freely from *Brevities*. And when they catch him at it, he is angry. He is at one and the same time feuding with *Brevities,* Louis Sobol, Harry Hershfield, Nita Naldi, Ed Sullivan, Emile Gauvreau, Paul Yawitz, and O. O. McIntyre.

But he is most sensitive about *Brevities.*

Brevities has everything that Winchell has, except the multi-million audience. The items are gossipy inside stuff.

The accuracy rate is much higher. The approach is bolder. The slang is better, less forced.

It was on the original *Brevities* in 1916 where O. O. McIntyre got his start.

On August 11, 1931, *Brevities* editor Tom Davin writes a "Personal Memorandum to W. W."

"I trust I am not over-presuming about your omniscience," he writes on *Brevities'* editorial page, "to warn you against unreliable tipsters in these Mondays of uncertainty. F'rinstance: Fifi d'Orsay isn't the only Dutch treater in the Beeway crowd. Helen Morgan is a good sport too."

Davin goes on to point out error after error in a single Winchell column. He cites a three-weeks old *Variety* as the source for some of the Winchell "scoops."

"The fact that the new Waldorf was to have a railroad siding was printed in Jeff Williamson's book: 'The American Hotel'—An Anecdotal History, just a year ago as well as the info that that caravansary is also wired for television in each suite."

On and on Davin goes, concluding finally with a parody of a then popular advertisement for an alleged halitosis remover: "Things like these, even your best friends won't tell you. But then . . . Yours, T.D."

Winchell becomes furious. *Brevities* then carries the blind item: "That Broadway columnist who used to spend his spare time signing phony names on libelous telegrams to his confreres is now occupying his leisure moments telling news-dealers what a lousy paper *Brevities* is."

Winchell is especially upset at one item which reports that the Matchabellis have filed a libel suit against the *Mirror* and Winchell.

The columnist denies that he has libeled the family. The suit for libel has been filed against the *Mirror*. Winchell has "defended" the Matchabellis on his broadcast.

With a hurt rebuff, he informs *Brevities:* "Obviously neither the Matchabellis and (sic) your reporter didn't hear my chatter on the air."

The final reprimand: "Get it right, Davin," Winchell writes in his letter to *Brevities*, "and when you don't get it right—try to correct a wrong assertion which is what I'm always doing."

Arthur Brisbane knows the vast circulation value to his *Daily Mirror* of Winchell's patter and innuendo. The real-estate tycoon considers Winchell a nuisance but a necessary one.

The only thing in the paper Brisbane seems to dislike more than Winchell is Mickey Mouse.

"Throw that rat out!" he shouts periodically at Emile Gauvreau.

Gauvreau fights for Mickey Mouse, and Winchell fights for Winchell. The columnist has asked for a large increase in salary to do a Sunday column. His column is appearing six days a week, and on Sunday the space is occupied by Paul Yawitz.

Yawitz writes a column similar to Winchell's though he occasionally takes the trouble to check the accuracy of his gossip.

Winchell's resentment grows. Maybe Brisbane is building up Yawitz to replace Winchell. Winchell watches with mounting jealousy as the *Sunday Mirror* circulation climbs without him. It reaches 1,300,000, thanks to the growing popularity of such color comics as Lil Abner.

Yawitz is beginning to be talked about as "another Winchell." Winchell on weekdays and Yawitz on Sundays.

A showdown is inevitable. Winchell visits Brisbane's office.

"A.B., I'm going to do a Sunday column."

"Walter, my boy," Brisbane says, "better you should read a good book on Sundays. You should read Thackery and Dickens."

"I'd like to start this week."

"Have you ever read a book?"

"Listen, A.B., I've decided to cut my price. I'll make it easy on you—"

"We don't want two columns on Sunday," Brisbane says.

"I'll do it cheap, boss."

"How cheap?"

Winchell says $165. This is about half of what the *Mirror* is paying Yawitz.

"Okey. I don't know what we'll do about Yawitz though."

"Get rid of him," Winchell says. "That's part of the deal."

On Sunday, Yawitz ends his column with his usual, ". . . Miss Feathersby, My Hat!"

In the words of Gauvreau: "Yawitz went down unceremoniously, after the manner of a general whose horse has been shot from under him."

On November 25th, the following week, Walter Winchell is the Sunday columnist.

This is the month in which he talks about seeing Larry Fay in Dinty Moore's restaurant. Remarkable to one and all inasmuch as Fay has been dead for two years, and, so far as anyone knows, has been safely buried so he cannot haunt or be haunted by a Winchell column.

The scene is Lindy's Restaurant on Broadway between 49th and 50th Streets. Winchell strolls from table to table, grunting hello, nodding recognition.

A tall, large, woman enters the restaurant. She walks directly to the columnist, coming up behind him. She turns him around on his heels.

"Mr. Winchell, do you know me?"

"What the hell—"

"You don't know me, do you."

"All right, so I don't know you. So what?"

"So this," she says, swinging a lively right hand and

slapping him in the face with all her might. He rocks on his feet and stands gaping at her, stunned.

The woman turns and leaves.

Restaurant owner Leo Lindeman hurries over. "Walter, I like you. You're a nice boy. But I've told you I'll have absolutely no fighting in my establishment."

"Who is she?" Winchell mutters to nobody in particular.

"That's Nita Naldi," someone says from a nearby table. She was the heroine in Rudolph Valentino's flickers.

Then he remembers. He has written that she is broken down and in a sanitarium in France. He has hinted that she is taking dope.

"Jeez," he mutters, rubbing his reddened cheek. "I'm lucky she didn't kill me. I'll get that bitch."

See him as they saw him then.

Winchell telling his brother not to bother him: "I'm an important man now, Al. I don't want you hanging around."

He sends money to his mother by mail. He sends her movie passes. But he orders her not to come to the house to visit her grandchildren.

"It upsets June when you come around," he writes.

To a friend he confides that his mother's Jewish accent embarasses him.

She later commits suicide. She'd undergone a depressing fit of loneliness.

Neighbors at her rooming house are surprised to learn that she was the mother of Walter Winchell.

"She never mentioned it. Not even once," her landlady says.

A check reveals that she has received no visitors for more than six weeks before her breakdown and suicide plunge.

On her bureau, police find a poem Winchell had written to her when he was still with *Vaudeville News*. "Lines

To A Lady" is the title, and it bears the subtitle, "My Mother":

> The silver hairs that streak the locks you own
> Are signs of cares caused by the seeds I've sown;
> Sad silent symbols of your hours alone;
> Remainders of the bitterness you've known.
>
> You'd rather smile than grumble or complain
> When my neglect and thoughtlessness was plain;
> You suffered silently, and all in vain,
> Oh how I wish I hadn't caused you pain.

The funeral is a quiet affair. Winchell doesn't attend.

18

The Errors of His Ways

In 1953 Washington newsmen coined a new word. They were probably thinking of Walter Winchell. The word was "psychoceramic." It was intended to describe unreliable sources who peddle tips that are more dramatic than accurate.

In the course of a pre-trial hearing of a libel suit against Winchell, the columnist candidly admitted that he dealt in rumor.

"I collect news," he testified, "and offer it to the papers, all kinds of news. In earlier years it was a gossip column. It has always been gossip—I would call it that, yes. It covers almost everything. Nothing that interests me is outside my province."

"He believes," commented St. Clair McKelway for the *New Yorker* magazine, "that if a thing is true, or even half true, it is material for his column . . ."

McKelway wrote a five-part profile of Winchell for the *New Yorker*. With the assistance of John Bainbridge, he checked for accuracy five Monday columns which Winchell published in the month of April, 1940.

Of 239 items, 108 had to be dropped from the test because they contained no names or because the names they contained were of people who wouldn't discuss the matter, or because they were merely items of opinion.

This left 131 items, which were checked.

McKelway found 53 items to be completely accurate,

24 to be partly inaccurate, and 54 to be completely inaccurate.

This meant that far fewer than fifty percent of Winchell's items were accurate.

McKelway also examined thoroughly Winchell's claims as a reporter on the Lindbergh baby kidnapping and the subsequent trial and conviction of Bruno Richard Hauptman.

Winchell had claimed 19 scoops.

McKelway found of the 19, only two were scoops, and these had "qualifications." One scoop was never confirmed, and so according to McKelway, "it was hardly a scoop."

Two so-called scoops were stories that appeared the same day in other papers. Six so-called scoops had appeared in the *New York Times* four to six days earlier. Seven so-called scoops couldn't be considered scoops in any sense of the word since they were not news beats of any kind, and one so-called scoop was a case where Winchell had misquoted his own editor.

A few years later a group of newsmen having a beer at the Newspaper Guild bar on West 43rd Street in New York, decided to build a pool to be awarded to the person who found the most errors in a Winchell column during a four week period. They collected $27.

To make it more difficult, they agreed that the errors would have to be consecutive errors, in that one must follow the other without an accurate item intervening.

The bartender, who apparently had more time to pursue the Winchell column than the newspaper reporters, won the money, having been an original contributor to the pool.

He had found four consecutive items in a column that were factually untrue. If Winchell hadn't interspersed a plug for Winchell, the bartender might have rung up a string of six, since two more followed immediately thereafter.

Rarely did anything interest Winchell enough for him to work at getting his facts right on it.

He was likely as not to be wrong even about himself. On two separate occasions he announced the forthcoming birth of a new little Winchell. Both times he later retracted. These were two of the very few times he ever gave a straightforward retraction.

The man who in his prime was producing hundreds of "facts" a day for the three-hundred daily newspapers then carrying his column, was not even sure of the date of his own marriage, which he listed in Biographical Encyclopedia as 1922 and in Current Biography as 1923.

Even when accurate facts were sent him, he was liable to botch them up. Thus a telegram saying that "So-and-so was hired to edit the new *Music Business* magazine for $25,000 a year for five years and given a $5,000 bonus on signing the contract," was garbled in the WW column to read: "At $130,000 per annum."

Now, it is doubtful if there is an editor in the United States who receives $130,000 a year. It is certainly doubtful if a new little trade paper would be in a position to pay its editor a salary greater than the total salaries of eight Senators.

Important people were wary of asking for retractions, for Winchell usually phrased these in such a way as to do more harm than the original error.

Many of the early Winchell columns read like fairy tales to the people who were mentioned in them. It was often said that being unable to get enough inside news on celebrities, Winchell made some of it up. At least, until he established his personal coterie of camp followers among press agents.

His errors were like confetti. A random selection could be made by any reader who studied a Winchell column a week or more old.

This didn't bother Winchell. On one of his two meetings with William Randolph Hearst he was chided by the old man for the way his fingertips at a typewriter played havoc with facts.

"Look at it this way, Chief," he is reported to have said. "If I say Trixie Friganza is vacationing in New York, and she hasn't been out of California for years, I'm wrong, right? But by the time the reader can be sure I'm wrong he's already reading tomorrow's column. Besides, my errors are little ones."

After his first meeting with Winchell, Hearst told his secretary: "He seems to satisfy the whims of our readers, but I don't like the man. I don't want to see him again, ever. Keep him far away from me."

On another occasion Hearst sent a wire to his editors which said:

PLEASE EDIT WINCHELL VERY CAREFULLY AND LEAVE OUT ANY DANGEROUS OR DISAGREEABLE PARAGRAPHS. INDEED, LEAVE OUT THE WHOLE COLUMN WITHOUT HESITATION, AS I THINK HE HAS GOTTEN SO CARELESS THAT HE IS NO LONGER OF ANY PARTICULAR VALUE.

It wasn't so much that Winchell was wrong that fascinated newspaper professionals. Or even that he was so often wrong when he could have been right if he'd invested a nickel in a telephone call.

It was how consistently wrong he was. And often, when feuding with an imaginary or real enemy, how deliberately wrong he was.

The *New York Post* once compiled a file of what they called "Walter's WWrongos." The men who did the compiling were able to find, with ease, at least fifty obvious errors in every Monday column.

Some of the Winchell errors were comical, some trite, some treacherous.

Eleven times in eleven months he announced that Norma Shearer would play Scarlett O'Hara in "Gone

With The Wind." Then, on the radio and in his column, he dramatically announced that the prediction he made "sixty-five weeks ago" about Norma Shearer playing Scarlett O'Hara had just been officially confirmed.

Vivienne Leigh played Scarlett O'Hara.

Usually more than half of the items in any Winchell column were wrong. If Winchell mentioned that a couple were about to be married, they may have been married six months before. Or they may have each been married to other mates a week ago.

If Winchell mentioned that actress Eva Gabor was seen walking down Fifth Avenue with her poodle, the chances are fifty-fifty that she hadn't been in New York for a month and that she never had a poodle in her life and may in fact be allergic to dogs.

Meander through a Winchell column.

Item:

Gloria Swanson couldn't have secretly married B. Brent in Mexico months ago like they are rumoring?

She could have, but she didn't. Never met the gentleman. Never heard of him before his name appeared in the column.

Item:

Eartha Kitt's recording "Uska Dara" has the nightingale chanting Turkish lyrics. Smarty pants note: Uskudar is the name of a town in Turkey.

You don't have to be a "smarty pants" to know that Uskudar is the name of a town in Turkey. You merely have to listen to the lyric, which tells you so.

Item:

Locals expect the Postmaster-General's resignation before July.

It didn't happen.

Item:

Insiders say Ike's speeches are designed by C. D. Jackson's dept.

Correct. But the news in Winchell's column appeared almost a year after the story of ghostwriter Jackson had

been told in full by *Time, Life, Newsweek, The Nation*
and many others.

Item:

**The zaniest new song is the Dagmar-Sinatra platter called
"Mama Will Bark!"**

This one appeared one and one-half years after
the Dick Manning song creation had been released by
Columbia Records. Manning couldn't understand the
plug; says the record was the most resounding flop he
ever wrote. The hit songwriter thinks Dagmar and Sina-
tra would agree.

Item:

**Conrad Hilton, the hotel magnate, is the latest bitten by the
political bug. His campaign will be launched soon . . .**

Hilton's comment to the author: "I haven't been bitten
by anything since I started stopping at Hilton hotels."

Item:

The Adam Powells (Hazel Scott) are weighing a problem.

They didn't know about any problem but hoped Winchell could enlighten them.

Item:

**The Jack Bennys are grumbling. Not over their long-time happy
merger. She wants him to quit show biz; Jake says nope.**

Mrs. Benny's comment: "The only grumbling around
here is the sound of Winchell's column being digested
by our new automatic garbage disposal unit."

Item:

**The background music for the "Ruby Gentry" cinema should
be recorded. A fascinating tempo that toys with the heartstrings.**

The music had been recorded four months before, and
on the day the Winchell suggestion appeared, the music
was number one on the nation's song hit parade.

Item:

**Whittaker Chambers, former Russian top U.S. spy (while senior
editor at Time mag), is back on the payroll.**

Winchell didn't say whose payroll. Chambers wasn't on *Time*'s payroll. Maybe Winchell meant the payroll of the Russian secret police.

Item:

> Justice Learned Hand denied our recent tip—that he would soon leave the Fed bench. The controversy that followed was over the word "resign." We didn't say "resign." We said retirement . . . He'll probably retire in June.

But a check of back columns reveals that Winchell did say "resign." Hand did retire. Two years, one month and twenty-three days later. The judge was 83 years old.

Winchell had a quaint way of making corrections. His retractions were invariably barbed with resentment.

When Winchell wrote on January 26, 1942, that "Ruth Sato, the Eurasian entertainer (half Japanese—half Yankee Doodle) will change her name to Pearl Haba," Miss Sato was more than a little angry.

She demanded a retraction under threat of a law suit. Winchell complied with:

> Ruth Sato, the American-born Eurasian entertainer, denies she is changing her name to Pearl Haba.

Ruth Sato's name never appeared in another Winchell column.

On another occasion, Winchell reported that a certain crooner was hanging around with parlor pinks.

Pressed for a retraction, he wrote: "(soandso) says he isn't a red."

Whether he was reporting that "Sinclair Lewis will play the lead in a new play William Saroyan is writing for the Theatre Guild" or "FDR will announce that he isn't going to seek a third term any day now" Winchell never bothered to check with the people he was writing about. Or even to check with their press agents.

You couldn't accuse him of being partial. If he didn't check with Sinclair Lewis or William Saroyan or the Theatre Guild or President Roosevelt or the President's press secretary—well then, he didn't check with his own wife.

On March 12, 1951, he reported:

Mrs. W. Winchell is in the hospital with agonizing bursitis.

Two weeks later on March 26, he wrote:

Mrs. Winchell is mending rapidly. The various miracle drugs almost killed her.

Three days after that on March 29, he wrote:

Mrs. W. says no miracle drugs hurt her. That ACTH is all the scientists say it is. The anesthetics were the villains. (Veddy soddy, moddom).

The little trite lies he told in the thirties were nothing as compared to the whoppers yet to come.

In April of 1953, he led off his column with this blind item:

Tragedy for a great movie star. Doctors ordered her to retire. Cancer.

No names.

On May 10th on his broadcast, Winchell sounded as if he had just uncovered the Pulitzer Prize story of the century when he announced on both his radio and television show that Bette Davis was in Memorial Hospital in New York with cancer and that a party planned in her honor had to be called off. He also carried the story in his Monday column.

This was a typical Winchell "scoop."

Except that Bette Davis didn't have cancer. The party which had been called off was called off because she had an infected tooth. She wasn't in Memorial Hospital. She wasn't even in New York at the time of the Winchell broadcast.

Other newspapers checked the story and discovered the Winchell fabrication.

Her husband told a newspaperman: "We never listen to Winchell or read him. At least we haven't for many years. The whole thing came as a surprise when telephone calls began coming in from our friends."

To another newspaperman he complained: "It's frightening—the explaining that's got to be done. Why didn't Winchell call the hospital and find out if Bette was there? I haven't even called Winchell to give him the true story. His retractions are worthless."

Winchell ignored the matter for an entire week.

Finally, he carried the text of a telegram he'd received from the actress:

YOUR RECENT STATEMENTS ABOUT ME ARE UTTERLY WITHOUT FOUNDATION. HAVE AUTHORIZED MY PHYSICIAN AT NEW YORK HOSPITAL TO ANSWER ANY QUESTIONS YOU MAY CARE TO PUT TO HIM, AND TO EXAMINE HOSPITAL'S AND PATHOLOGISTS REPORTS. I AM SURE YOU HAVE NO WISH TO HURT ME. ACCEPT MY ASSURANCES THAT I DO NOT HAVE CANCER. PLEASE RETRACT.—BETTE DAVIS.

Commented Winchell:

The happiest retraction in my 32 years on the papers.

Miss Ethel Barrymore, writing a note of sympathy to Bette Davis, commented: "I've been saying it for lo these many years. I don't see why that vulture Winchell has been allowed to live."

19

The Green Years

The high years in Winchell's life were exciting and eventful.

Winchell gained his widest syndication when as many as 430 newspapers printed one or more of his columns each week.

He became the most-listened to news commentator in the history of radio. For a number of years his Sunday 9 P.M. broadcast was the most widely heard radio program in America. It outranked the broadcasts of the most popular comedians, dramatic shows and music variety programs.

It was not unusual at club meetings, union meetings or social gatherings for someone to say, "It's almost nine. Let's hear Winchell." And for fifteen minutes everything would stop while a radio was turned on.

He wrote articles for fancy literary magazines like *The Bookman*. His favorable comments about any movie or play were widely reproduced on billboards and in newspapers throughout the country. His comment on an act would be clipped and given page one prominence in the act's scrapbook. (It didn't seem to matter that Winchell had never actually seen the movie, play or act.)

Time magazine carried his picture on its cover.

Getting one's name in Winchell's column became a goal to some that ranked almost as high in import as for instance, getting married.

A debutante (Winchell called them "debutramps")

held a party at Jack White's "18 Club" on 52nd Street, to celebrate her getting her name in Winchell's column.

"You've finally broken in, kid," her escort said, in proposing a toast. "You've made it. Are you happy?"

"Oh I'm the most," she said. "The very most."

A press agent named Art Franklin reported that a manufacturer had offered him $5,000 if Franklin could secure a one-line mention of the man's company in Winchell's column.

Franklin rejected the offer with a flip: "Winchell doesn't go for anything commercial like that."

Popular songwriters included lines in their songs like "Winchell linked me with you," and "I didn't know that we were through, I didn't know that I'd be blue, then Winchell Reno-vated us today . . ."

Hollywood made two movies with Winchell as a co-star. One was called "Love and Hisses" and the other "Wake Up and Live." Other films were made in which the protagonist was obviously Winchell. Winchell sold a "plot treatment" to a film studio, for which he received $25,000, though the story was never filmed.

He quietly went on the payroll of Twentieth-Century-Fox studios, and did at least one trailer for that studio praising a film. For this, Winchell received $5,000. It apparently didn't occur to Winchell or the Fox studios that there might be something unethical in buying the columnist's favorable comment. Winchell never bothered, before or after the trailer, to see the film he had praised.

Although before the elections of 1932, he expressed some disdain for both Hoover and Roosevelt, he became a Roosevelt fan during the famous "first hundred days" of the FDR administration.

Roosevelt wasn't a very frequent reader of the Winchell column but he was aware of its influence and wide audience.

At a strategy meeting of top New Dealers, Roosevelt is reported to have made the decision to use Winchell as a sounding board.

The President explained that it might be possible to feel out public sentiment toward a project before such a project was officially announced, if a couple of rumors about it were planted in Winchell columns.

Robert Sherwood, one of Roosevelt's ghost-writers, objected strongly.

"Winchell," said Sherwood, in his fine clipped English, "is a man who dwells in cabaret cellars. A little gray mouse, always hunting for cheese."

Others who were present convinced him of Winchell's value. It was decided to use Winchell.

Roosevelt had properly measured the columnist as a man easily swayed by a little flattery. The President wrote a letter to Winchell thanking him for his "support." A phone call, in which Roosevelt commented laughingly on a gag Winchell had published, was enough to clinch the deal.

The Winchell column thus took on its first political coloration.

Simon and Schuster asked Winchell to do a book for them. He agreed, signed a contract, and accepted an advance to write "The Private Papers of Walter Winchell." However, for practical reasons, his ghost writers seemed glum about the book. Even if it were possible to work plugs for their clients into a book, by the time the book appeared, the clients may have become ex-clients.

Winchell returned the advance to the book publisher.

Ben Bernie, an orchestra leader, developed a light-hearted friendly "feud" with Winchell, after both men agreed it would be good publicity for each of them.

Until the orchestra leader died, the two men would take humorous slaps at each other on their broadcasts, in the manner of the Jack Benny-Fred Allen or Bob Hope-Bing Crosby feuds.

Winchell developed his friendship with FBI Director J. Edgar Hoover, and seriously proposed that cloak and dagger man as a Presidential candidate for the Democrats.

At this point, it would be well to see Winchell in whole focus as he appeared in the late nineteen-thirties and the early nineteen-forties.

He was the most widely read columnist the world had ever known.

He was the most listened to radio commentator—the most listened to regular radio program—ever to appear on American network radio.

He was a friend of the President of the United States, of the Director of the Federal Bureau of Investigation, of the top gang leaders in America.

He was an emperor in the entertainment field. Mention in his column was sought by executor and executed alike.

His praise could make a play the critics had damned. ("Hellzapoppin"). His endorsement could sell thousands of copies of a book. ("Plot Against The Peace"—written by men he later reluctantly identified as "two Communists.")

He had wealth, estimated at between two and three million dollars. He had prestige. He had women. He had power.

Winchell was in his prime.

As an article in *Collier's* magazine remarked: "No other performer has ever done so well with so little."

20

The Lone Ranger Rides

"This Waldo Winchester," wrote Damon Runyon in a short story called "Romance in the Roaring Forties,"—"this Waldo Winchester is a nice-looking young guy who writes pieces about Broadway for the *Morning Item.* He writes about the goings-on in night clubs, such as fights, and one thing and another, and also about who is running around with who, including guys and dolls.

"Sometimes this is very embarrassing to people who may be married and are running around with people who are not married, but of course Waldo Winchester cannot be expected to ask one and all for their marriage certificates before he writes his pieces for the paper."

Winchell was hardly the hero of the story, for "Waldo Winchester" is justifiably beaten up, is engaged to a girl even while he is married to another, and so forth.

Runyon at this time had frequently expressed something which might at best be called disdain for Winchell. Sometimes the columns of both men appeared on the same page.

It is typical of Runyon that he didn't read Winchell's column. He preferred the classics or old copies of Brann's *Iconoclast.*

It is typical of Winchell that he needed to believe that everybody read his column.

The New Yorker reported that a friend of Winchell had not seen the column on a certain Tuesday. Winchell wanted to know if the friend had been ill.

Another time another friend returned to New York after a trip to Europe. "Jeez, Walter," he said, "I sure did miss the column. I didn't see it for two whole weeks."

"That's all right," Winchell is said to have replied, "You can go over to the *Mirror* office tomorrow and look at the files."

A clue to the fear that everybody was *not* reading him might be found in his policy of sending marked photostats of his column to people whose favor he sought, when he happened to mention them.

The fear was justified, in the case of Damon Runyon.

One of the most popular of the Runyon stories was Madame La Gimp. It was transformed into a film titled "Lady for a Day" which won three Academy Awards.

The heroine of the story was a broken down fruit seller whom Runyon called Apple Annie. When the film was made, Apple Annie received some money from Hollywood.

A few years later, however, she starved to death.

Winchell had actually written in his column that she was starving. When she died, the *Herald-Tribune* mentioned that Winchell had revealed that she was in a state of starvation ten days previous to her death.

"Did you see that scoop I had on Apple Annie?" Winchell asked Runyon when the two met that night at the Stork Club.

"What scoop?" Runyon asked. He was feeling melancholy about the death of the old woman whose story had brought so much fame to him.

"Why I called the shot two weeks ago," Winchell said. "Even the Trib gave me credit for that one. I knew the old lady was on her way out."

"You had that in your column?" Runyon said, incredulously.

"Sure. Here. Look," and Winchell held the original column up for Runyon.

"Why didn't you do something about it, Walter," said

Runyon, becoming angry. "A couple of dollars worth of warm soup might have saved her life."

"I'm no charity clinic," Winchell said. "Why didn't you do something about it."

"Because I didn't know," Runyon replied testily. "Because I don't read your God-damned column." With that he walked from the restaurant, not even bothering to stop for his hat.

For months the two men didn't talk. Runyon would avoid Winchell whenever possible. And yet, at last, they became friendly again. When a collection of short stories including "Madame La Gimp" was scheduled to appear in 1942, Winchell talked Runyon into allowing him to write the introduction.

Winchell could never understand why the respect he was willing to accord Runyon wasn't a mutual thing.

"He possesses all the necessary attributes that go to make the guy the rest of us on the staff wish we were," Winchell once wrote of Runyon.

Of Winchell, Runyon wrote to a friend: "I don't dislike Walter. He is a mixture of comedy and pathos that make him enjoyable company for me in my dotage."

When Runyon's throat cancer deprived him of his voice, he would speak through a pencil and pad which he carried around in his hands like a pair of gloves.

Often when listening to Winchell, Runyon would scribble a note. Winchell would glance at it without interrupting his own flow of talk.

By accident, Runyon once held the pad so that the writing was upside down. Winchell nodded, said, "I know," and continued talking. This so amused Runyon that he would frequently turn the pad upside down as a practical joke.

Only rarely would Winchell discover the prank.

"Walter admires me because I can't talk back," Runyon wrote on his pad. "I'm his captive audience."

It was Runyon who coined the classic Broadway line, "Winchell never forgets a favor, if he did it . . ."

Although Winchell concentrated most of his columning on celebrities, he often expressed his own distaste for being around them. They made him feel uneasy.

"I spend no more time with them than I can help," he once told a magazine interviewer. "I just don't like celebrities . . ."

At another time he remarked: "Some people might say I don't go around with celebrities because I want to be the center of attraction myself. But that isn't true. I hate and avoid all cocktail parties, receptions and banquets . . . I never entertain anybody. Nobody ever entertains me. I like my privacy."

When J. P. McEvoy was chatting with Winchell for *Saturday Evening Post*, Winchell warned him, "You keep my family out of this."

"But Walter," McEvoy said, "you've made a national reputation and a tremendous fortune out of other people's private affairs."

"That's different," Winchell said. "That's business."

"But this is business too," McEvoy insisted. "How can I write about you if I don't know something about your interest outside your work?"

"I haven't any interests outside my work."

Later, when McEvoy telephoned Winchell's office, he was told by the secretary, "I can't give out any information about Winchell."

"Does he work here?" McEvoy asked.

"I can't say."

"When did you see him last?"

"I don't remember," the secretary replied, and hung up.

The secretary was Rose Bigman. She tried to copy Winchell's arrogance and snippiness. When she called other offices and the secretaries would ask if they could help her, secretary Bigman would snap: "Put your boss on. Bigman doesn't speak to secretaries. Bigman speaks to bosses."

Winchell exploited Irving Hoffman's keen knowledge of the libel law. Other press agents also suggested word marriages that would help avoid court action, and soon his readers were reading words and phrases like "telling it to a judge," "soured," "curdled," "in husband trouble," and "this and that way" as substitutes for divorced or going to be divorced.

Nevertheless, the staccato prose didn't race quite fast enough to avoid all legal entanglements.

Winchell always tried to keep out of the way of publicity about the libel cases he lost, and there were many of them.

Once he referred to someone as a "rat." He could have called the man a mouselike creature without libelling him, but not a "rat." The *Daily Mirror* made a cash settlement.

In another instance he wrote that a certain beach club was a "racket." The next day so many members withdrew that the club went bankrupt. The club sued, and Winchell's paper was hit for $30,000. This later was reduced, after legal appeals, to $15,000.

In 1939 he wrote that merchant seamen who were members of the National Maritime Union were using mercury and emery dust to sabotage ships. The union sued and collected $19,000. It used the money to finance leadership training schools for members.

Under questioning, Winchell once admitted that he was "at that moment" defending himself in five libel actions.

Two, which had gotten to court a few months earlier had cost his newspaper what was described as "a sum equal to about a month of Winchell's salary."

There have been numerous other settlements.

One was to a midwestern farmer who claimed his reputation had been damaged when Winchell wrote that he got out on the limb of a tree and sawed the limb from the tree so that he fell to the ground.

Actually, Winchell has a unique arrangement with his

newspaper and with his radio network, whereby they assume all liability for his statements.

They and not he have to pay out when he loses a libel suit.

The result is that everything he writes is edited not only by an editor—but by a lawyer as well.

Winchell has always been beneficiary of fortunate circumstance in that for self-protective reasons, newspapers have been very reluctant about publicizing libel suits or the grounds for libel. The result is that only one person out of a thousand who *could* sue Winchell, knows enough about his rights to even consider suing Winchell.

Tireless and tormented by an unappeasable itch for fame and power, Winchell was the unchallenged King of the Gossip Columnists by the mid-thirties.

Hy Gardner had written a long time before in *Zit's* "The moment we start collecting choice bits of gossip and shaping them into a column, we must involuntarily but obviously pattern our patter after Winchell . . ."

There were many imitators, but there was only one Winchell.

Gardner, like many other new columnists, easily fell within the Winchell sphere of influence.

The new columnist would be surprised and delighted by a pleasant note from Winchell with words to the effect that the new column was "great." Another note or two containing appreciative sentiments would follow.

This "thoughtfulness" paid off for Winchell in two ways.

For one thing, it was highly unlikely that the newcomer would now say anything unkind about his "friend" and "admirer" Walter Winchell. The notes were thus a safety precaution.

But there was greater method to Winchell's means.

If anyone dared to criticize Winchell, he could now fight back by indirection. He would drop another note to the newcomer and say, "Do me a favor and carry this line, will you?" and suggest a line to "kill" an enemy.

That way, Winchell seemingly avoided replying to his critics even while they were pelted from many other directions.

Columnists like Gardner, Frank Farrell of the *World-Telegram,* Jack O'Brian of the *Journal-American,* Nick Kenny of the *Daily Mirror* and others were easy prey for this strategy.

Also, when Winchell wanted to "start a campaign" as in the case of his fiasco against dialect comedians, he would write, "You can do something for me by supporting this," to the columnists. Then, when everybody would seem to join in, he would take bows for beginning the thing and leading the way.

People who claimed to know him well were saying that he was still running, still frightened, still worried that he wouldn't be able to stay on top.

But he had reasons. He had watched others fall quickly from the top into the discard pile. Statesmen, actors, sport champions, singers, literary celebrities— he'd written about them all—and he'd watched many of them topple and flounder in the decay of their own lost popularity.

A woman who had known, encouraged, and befriended Winchell wrote: "There was something so pitiful about this man—fabulously successful in a worldly sense, abysmally unsuccessful as a human being."

But to most gossip-column readers, Winchell was "the one." At his peak an estimated twenty-five million people read Winchell every day except Saturday. Few questioned the authenticity of anything he wrote.

Winchell was a man who "knew all the big shots" and readers imagined that the big shots whispered their intimate secrets to him on some cozy dark street or at post-midnight breakfasts in their penthouse castles.

Mostly however, it was the press agents who paid homage to Winchell at his club.

The item was an innocuous one in the Monday column. He wrote on November 9, 1934:

I hear Sherman Billingsley is reviving the old Stork Club, and that's gay news. For that spot's atmosphere has never been matched even by Sherman in his newer rendezvous . . .

Thus did Winchell herald the return of convicted felon Billingsley to the Winchell sphere of influence.

Billingsley was a front man for the so-called mob and whatever else he was, Winchell was respectful toward the gun-bearers of Manhattan.

Billingsley and Winchell were quick to get together in an arrangement to benefit both men.

Winchell was permitted unlimited cuffo (free supply) of food and drink for himself and his friends. He would be assigned a private table, permanently reserved for him.

Naturally, Winchell would pepper his column with plugs for the Stork Club. Of some importance to Billingsley too was the fact that Winchell agreed never to mention Billingsley's criminal background. More important, he was never to mention Billingsley's previous marriage.

Winchell kept his word.

The table he selected was "table 50," from where he could view everything and everybody in the notorious "Cub Room."

Once, when too many gangsters were being murdered in barbershops, Winchell spoke to Billingsley, who immediately built a private barber shop in the club so that Winchell could have his hair cut in safety.

In return, Winchell plugged the club in column after column. It became apparent that if one wanted one's name in Winchell's column, one's chances would improve greatly if one were seen at the Stork Club.

The Stork Club became "the place to go" and Winchell became a Stork Club fixture.

21

Why Columnists Die Young

Some toil at night to make the grade—
To fill the space for which they're paid—
Or try to pen a grin or laugh
In every other paragraph:
Or string some words to make a verse
Which helps to fill a lanky purse,
When some chump yap chirps in rebuff
"Say! Do you really write this stuff?"

WALTER WINCHELL

The cocky arrogant Winchell headed his column of September 25, 1924, "WE HATE TO BRAG"— and wrote:

In justice to the followers of this pillar of gab we regret that limited space forces us to crowd out 1,500 columns of press agent material. Apologies to the Times and News.

Suggesting, of course, that the *Times* and *News* were using press agent material and he wasn't.

Actually, Winchell was being deceptive, for even then he depended on the expanding army of press agents for most of his material.

(He preferred to refer to them as his "field representatives.")

As the years went by, Winchell did less and less news-gathering himself.

His "news" consisted of material, in large part rumors, which was supplied to him daily by the press agents.

Many of them were able to earn $400 and $500 a week

by being able to deliver Winchell plugs on schedule for an act, a show, a recording, a book.

The press agents did nothing to discourage the belief that they had a "private wire" to Winchell and enjoyed his special favor.

Irving Hoffman was known to the public. Others who were "close" to Winchell's affections included press agents Ed Weiner, Kurt Weinberg, Howie Horwitz and Frank Law.

Those who were leaders in public relations like Steve Hannigan, Tom Fizdale, and other top money-men didn't bother with the Winchell column because they didn't consider it important.

When Winchell attended his broadcast, sat at his "table 50" at the Stork Club, or went on his post-midnight romps, it was usually press agents he'd surround himself with.

Ed Weiner, who spent night after night with Winchell once complained to friends that "I can't stand it any longer. He never wants to sleep. I'm going to crack up. I get home in the morning when my wife is getting up."

When the friends asked him why he didn't quit, Weiner replied: "I don't have the guts to stop." Then he broke into a weary smile, "Listen, five more years of this and I'll be able to retire for life."

But more than five years later, Weiner stopped *Daily News* radio editor Ben Gross and press agent Ivan Black in front of Reuben's Restaurant.

"I need some advice," Weiner said. "What am I gonna do about Winchell?"

Gross was sympathetic. "What's the trouble, Ed?"

Weiner shuddered. "Listen," he said, "I'm not a dog. I'm a human being."

"I know," Gross said.

"I don't have to go on this way. I've got fifty grand in the bank. What do you think? You think I ought to get out?"

"That's your decision. You have to make your own decision on something like that, Ed. Nobody can give you advice."

"Decision, hell. I'm gonna tell that son of a bitch where he gets off once and for all."

But despite the occasional outbursts, Weiner remained a faithful sheepdog, trailing Winchell around, dusting off his seat, yessing him, running for cold water when Winchell was thirsty.

Weiner's close relationship with Winchell was made necessary because as a press agent, he seemed to lack any real flair for writing. On some occasions his press releases were considered so preposterous that they were tacked on the bulletin board at the *Billboard* as bad examples.

Winchell was propped up by his ghostwriters, and some of the scheme of things rubbed off on Weiner.

In 1948, Longmans, Green and Co., published a book called "The Damon Runyon Story."

Weiner had supplied some fugitive notes and had done some research, but the bulk of the writing and editing was done by Pulitzer Prize poet Audrey Wurdemann and her husband, poet-novelist Joseph Auslander. These two ghostwriters went the silent unappreciated way of all good ghostwriters when the book was published.

For it bore the byline, "by Ed Weiner."

Although the book was allegedly the biography of Runyon, Weiner made sure that the real hero came through as Walter Winchell.

Yet, Weiner required an outlet for the hostility he felt toward the man who had lured him into an upsidedown world by dangling the bitch goddesses Success and Money before him.

And so Weiner wrote as he had never written before, fired by his own antagonism. He worked long and hard, and when he was through, he had written a full-length biography of Walter Winchell.

It wasn't flattering.

Only two of Weiner's intimate friends were permitted

to read it. His wife read it. And night after night Weiner mentioned it to Winchell.

The columnist showed no apparent interest; didn't ask to see the manuscript.

Finally one night as the two men were leaving the Stork Club at three a.m., Weiner thrust an envelope into Winchell's hands.

"This is that book about you," he said. "I want to know what you think."

Winchell read it, and told Weiner what he thought.

What he thought and what he said were enough to cause Weiner to "retire" the manuscript without its ever being submitted to a publisher or ever being shown to another human being.

This was the sheep dog's single bark back.

Hoffman, on the other hand, was the only press agent who talked back regularly. "Listen you jerk," he'd say to Winchell on occasion, "you're blowing your top. Now cool off."

Winchell was never as shocked at these outbursts as the people around him.

The press agents fawned upon Winchell like jesters in a royal court. They traveled with him to his Sunday night broadcast and they traveled with him from the studio to the Stork Club. He referred to them as "my bodyguard."

That he also lacked some confidence in them was evidenced by the fact that he carried two guns. He went about with a loaded automatic in his suit coat and another in his overcoat pocket.

He never shot a press agent.

The most difficult task facing press agents who wanted a steady flow of Winchell mentions for their clients was to provide complete columns for the master.

Other Broadway columnists would consider an idea for a column and approve or disapprove it. Winchell, however, insisted upon seeing the full finished column.

These were done on general things, away from the usual B'way gossip. They were full columns devoted to one subject or category like history or international affairs.

Since most press agents are busy people (spending much time convincing clients that they're getting "terrific" buildups) these Winchell columns were written by free lance writers, and newspapermen. Press agents paid varying rates for them ranging from $50 or $60 each to $300 if Winchell used the column.

Winchell, of course, paid nothing.

The columns were submitted to Winchell who returned those that didn't strike him. Then the press agents tried to pan them off on other columnists.

If Winchell used one out of five columns thus submitted, it was considered an excellent average. One film company press agent brags that Winchell once used two of his columns in a single week.

Winchell edited the material, giving it more zip and punch. But very rarely did he have to rewrite more than a paragraph or two inasmuch as the columns were already "Winchell styled."

In similar fashion he selected two or three hundred items for the Broadway gossip columns which appeared two or three times a week.

Winchell rarely read a book, saw a movie or attended a stage play opening night. He depended on press agents to feed him information on the value of any product in these three media.

For instance, Hoffman wrote the paragraphs on the week's new films that appeared in the Sunday column.

This didn't hurt Hoffman's standing with the film companies and he has been on more than one film company payroll for services performed.

The only way to actually get Winchell to look at anything in a book or magazine was to clip it open to the page you wanted him to see and mark the paragraphs.

If his name appeared in these paragraphs, chances of his mentioning the book or magazine were excellent.

The Winchell setup was not unique. More and more

Broadway columnists (Winchell called them "my imitators" and "the also-rans") came to depend almost entirely on press agents.

Westbrook Pegler once referred to Winchell as a "gent's room journalist" but neither Winchell nor the press agents who furnished most of what went into his column operated from the men's room. Rather, the press agents sat in their respective offices and spent an hour or two a day making telephone calls to people who "got around" and who might have seen someone or heard something that could be usable.

The press agents would also thumb through joke books, magazines like *Time* and *Newsweek,* and old columns by Ed Sullivan and Danton Walker who carried some of the same gossip.

Names were substituted for other names. Gags were lifted and given a twist. Facts were given so much "treatment" that they became fantasy by the time they were submitted to Winchell.

In desperation, a press agent would sometimes create important people for a series of items so the name of a client would be mentioned. Thus a press agent had as his client a dancer named Lynn Hale.

"Avant Keels, the Texas oil millionaire, will marry Lynn Hale any sundown," was the way the item would first appear in the column.

"Lynn Hale has stopped using soap. She gets richer suds using oil from the wells of Keels. That's Avant Keels," was the second.

"Avant Keels, the oil zillionaire, will bankroll a Broadway musical for his baby doll Lynn Hale, according to the rumor mongers," was the third.

The oil millionaire was an imaginary product of the press agent's mind, and he continued to supply imaginary items until enough real people items came along.

Other incidents requiring similar press agent-type ingenuity took place. For example, a press agent and a young *Variety* reporter were watching the electric light news ticker that travels around the Times Tower in Times Square.

The press agent began taking notes.

"What are you doing?" the reporter asked. "You can get all that stuff in the morning *Times* which will be out at eleven."

"I like it from the lights," the press agent said. "It's fresher and livelier. It stimulates me."

"What do you need it for?"

"You're not going to believe this, but two or three of the items I get off there will appear in Danton Walker's column in two weeks."

The reporter grinned. "I don't believe it. Doesn't Walker read the papers?"

"I won't argue with you," the press agent said, as he continued to copy. "Why should I tell you my trade secrets anyway."

After a pause, the reporter said, "You could never get away with that with Winchell."

"Wanna bet?"

The two men wagered five dollars on an item which they both agreed upon. Four days later the stale item appeared, with a slight twist, as a prediction in Winchell's column.

The reporter lost his bet.

There were some press agents who told intimates that they had finally figured out how to "handle" Winchell.

The trick was to avoid seeing him in person.

They would mail their material or send it to him by messenger. Every so often they would write a 'love note' telling him how 'terrific' yesterday's column was. When necessary, they would call him on the telephone to ask for overdue plugs.

But they would make special plans and take extra precautions not to meet him in the flesh.

If they saw him come into Lindy's, they would slip out through the employee's exit.

"Otherwise," as one explained, "he'd see you and you'd have to sit with him and maybe listen to him for hours, all the time saying to him only, 'Yes,' 'Yes,' and 'You're absolutely right, Walter.' And if while you sat there he happened to say, 'You know, your mother is a no good bitch,' you just had to say 'Yes,' and 'Yes, Walter,'—always agreeing with 'Yes, Walter,' and 'You said it, Walter.'

"Also, if you met him you were adding to the reasons he might find not to like you. The trick was not to meet him. You'd do better with him that way."

The importance of furnishing material to Winchell to get "a good in" was at one time so important that some high class industrial relations firms would hire an outside man for $75 or $85 a week. His job would be to accumulate items for Winchell, real or imaginary. These were sent to Winchell by the company. Unlike theatrical press agents, the company sought nothing immediate. It was merely that if a client needed a Winchell mention for vanity's sake, the company could promise to deliver.

The working relationship most press agents had with Winchell was a simple mathematical one.

The fringe group would deliver a daily batch of double-spaced typewritten items to his office at the *Daily Mirror*, from whence they would be forwarded by messenger boy.

The Winchell flock delivered the items directly to the desk of the Hotel St. Moritz.

Winchell would give an "orchid" or a rave plug for a press agent's client each time he was able to cull from the material five or more usable items that weren't about the client.

Press agents marked the items "for you" to indicate an

item on which they weren't profiting, and "for me" on an item plugging a client.

In his prime, Winchell would sometimes take generously from a press agent's submissions without coming forth with the plug.

If a press agent was unsure of his relationship, he might keep his unhappiness to himself.

Those who hovered on the inner circle however would write a brief plea that contained only the faintest trace of a whine, such as, "Dear Walter, What have I done wrong? You've used eleven items and not a mention of the Ink Spots. Please don't let me down, Walter. I need this client badly. If you are angry in any way with me, please let me know. And please don't be angry with this note."

Ten years after he had begun as a full-time daily newspaperman, Walter Winchell wrote about himself in *The Literary Digest:* "I don't golf, fish, swim, fly in planes, play piano, cook, or even ice skate."

When a hanger-on asked him why he didn't learn to fish or swim, Winchell stood looking at the friend, tight-lipped, skeptical, narrow-eyed.

"Listen," he said finally, with gruffness in his voice, "if I want to fish or swim, I don't have to learn. I'll send a press agent to do it for me."

Then he turned his back and walked away.

22

Winchell the Giant Killer

William Allen White once remarked that his conception of an ideal newspaper would be one which mentioned every one of its readers' names at least once in every issue.

A typical Winchell gossip column might contain three hundred items and name half that many people.

No newspaper could carry a Winchell column without losing something of its own personality. Before Winchell, some newspapers were snappy, some were dignified and some were dull.

The column fitted into the snappy papers naturally. It livened up the dull ones. And subtracted from the integrity of the dignified papers until they seemed like pompous men about to take a prat fall on a banana peel. No newspaper could retain its dreary ponderous impersonality when pervaded by a Winchell on any of its inner pages.

The Winchell column was the honey which seemed to attract the larger audience. And so the dignified papers offered a little less dignity in return for a little more circulation.

Winchell was profitable, but not always.

He cost the *Daily Mirror* an estimated sixty thousand dollars worth of theatrical advertising when he published a comparatively harmless story about Lee and Jake Shubert. He wrote that they were in the lobby of the Astor

Hotel mourning the closing of a play in which they had heavily invested.

The play's stage manager was with them, and when Jake moaned, "Why, oh why did we ever buy that guy's play?" the manager tried to console him with: "Don't take it too hard, boss, the Philadelphia Sesquicentennial didn't go over so hot either."

According to Winchell, Lee looked up startled and asked: "Did he write that too?"

The Shuberts were angry not merely because the story was fiction, but because they insisted Winchell knew it was fiction when he printed it.

So they cancelled the advertising for all Shubert shows and all Shubert-owned theatres.

It wasn't the first time that Winchell had tiffed with the real estate moguls.

Burned at some of Winchell's ribbing of their shows, the Shuberts ordered his name cut from their first nighter invitation list.

Winchell replied in his column: "If I can't go to the openings, I'll wait three days and go to the closings."

However, the face that launched a thousand quips was the front for the man who never forgot a slight or an unkind word.

Winchell actually memorized the unfavorable articles about himself which appeared in *The New Yorker*. For many years he could quote them word for word, and often did, to try to persuade whoever was around him that the articles had been unfair and untrue.

This was but a gentle breeze compared to the gale which broke loose in 1935 during the visit to New York of Dr. Alan Dafoe.

The old man had become a popular figure because of his delivery of the Dionne quintuplets.

After he'd been in town a few days, Dafoe was invited to attend a party in his honor tended by Mayor Frank Hague of Jersey City, New Jersey.

On the way to Jersey, a *New York Post* reporter over-heard Dafoe ask a friend: "Who is this man, Winchell, anyway? I never heard of him. Last night I was in a night club and he came over to my table and shook hands. He seemed to think he was important, so I thought he was."

The reporter used the quotation as an incidental part of the story only to illustrate how innocent and provincial Dafoe was.

Winchell's telegram to the *Post* was at least as long as the story.

He demanded to know the reason for the "intrigue" against him. He charged the *Post* with making a "violent and unprovoked" assault upon his good name. He warned that paper that if it was bent on ruining him, it could consider its own goose cooked.

He made outraged telephone calls.

His column was a volcano, spouting hate lava in the direction of the *Post's* managing editor, its publisher, its readers.

Not even Doctor Dafoe was to come away without being scorched. He sent Dafoe a bristling telegram, saying that if the *Post* report was true, the Doctor was unfit to hang around the little girls he "claimed" to have brought into the world. He demanded an immediate answer and a public apology from Dafoe.

Dafoe went back to Canada shaking his head over that "crazy man in the night club who has made such a fuss over so much nonsense."

He died some years later without ever having replied to Winchell's telegram, or a telegram sent to him by the *Post*.

An incident like the Dafoe slight was enough to enliven and embellish Winchell's natural bitterness for weeks at a time. During those periods he would howl like a dog passing razor blades.

And, as mentioned, he never forgot.

Once he told an editor at *Literary Digest,* "When I

used to tack up *The Daily News Sense* backstage at theatres, there were always some wise guys who would scribble smart remarks on the paper or tear it down. Some of those mugs now ask me for favors. They never get them."

He remembered too those movie critics who were less than enthusiastic about his advent into the motion picture world.

In 1937, his first starring film, "Wake Up and Live" was released nationally by Twentieth-Century-Fox. He was paid $75,000 for the role he played in the story, and spent at least a couple of hundred of those dollars on clipping services to get all the reviews appearing throughout the country.

The *Literary Digest* of April 17 forecast that "Winchell will go far as a movie star." At this time the *Digest* was dying from its forecast that Landon would defeat Roosevelt for the Presidency in 1936, so the Winchell prophesy could not have been the thing which doomed that magazine shortly thereafter.

The sequel was released one year later, in November, 1938. It was titled "Love and Hisses" and again starred Winchell and his friend Ben Bernie.

Newsweek's critic wrote that the film was "uninspired entertainment" but said that Winchell "shows progressive ability as an actor."

Winchell didn't win any academy awards, but he did clip the *Newsweek* review, showed it around to people in his usual modest way, referred to it in his column at least a dozen times and repeated the part about himself three times, lest any Winchell reader have failed to see it.

Time magazine was not as hopeful about Winchell's screen histrionics.

He never forgot, and never forgave. The only times he ever again mentioned *Time* with any warmth were on those occasions when he would quote from that magazine's overflattering statistics about his far reaching effect upon the American scene.

Thus when all the papers carrying the Winchell column had their circulations added together, the grand total was about 19,000,000. But when asked how many readers he had, Winchell would reply, "*Time* says 25,000,000."

On May 7, 1951, when Winchell was appearing in between 425 and 450 newspapers, many of them weeklies, Winchell was pleased to carry an item in his "Girl Friday" column saying: "*Time* says you now have 600 papers."

This was typical of the praise he showered upon himself with mounting frequency.

Any newspaper, magazine, book writer, radio performer or stage or screen personality could secure mention in Winchell's column by saying something pleasant about the columnist.

Once, he headed a column of such praise "Winchell the Magnificent," but syndicate editor Ward Greene suggested tactfully that he tone it down slightly. The column was headed instead: "Winchell the Great."

"It is silly to nurse bouquets," he wrote once. "They seem to sour with keeping. But if the world will take even the smallest thing you can give it—even one word of slang—that's a career—and an epitaph."

But the epitaphs that Winchell began to prefer were those of the people who offended him.

Now, most people prefer to keep out of trouble, to avoid controversy, arguments, fights. Not so, the growing Winchell. More and more, it seemed that he was content only if he was, as he himself put it in gangster vernacular, "giving someone the works."

"Did you see how I murdered that bum," he would ask, referring to an item in that day's column.

"He'll need a stretcher after this one," he said of one "enemy" after "giving him the works" in a one-sentence workout.

If Winchell's friends sometimes comprised a strange assortment, his enemies were equally odd.

From 1948 on, Winchell hated the Duke and Duchess of Windsor, apparently because they refused to fulfill his prediction that their marriage would break up.

At least once a month he would slap at the Windsors, jab at them, spit at them, scorn them, ridicule them.

But the Windsors wouldn't break up.

A sample of the persistence with which he has kept after the "prediction" may be found in the similarity of the items. In July, 1949, he wrote: "The Windsors are delaying that announcement to make WW look loony. But he'll have the last tee-hee. The lifted pinky set says the blowup will be any edition now."

Three years later, in August, 1952, he led off his column with: "The International Loafer Set expects the Windsor Thing to blow sky-high."

None of this tended to endear him to the Windsors.

In Norman Lockridge's book "Lesé Majesty," Duchess Wallis Windsor is quoted as complaining to her husband about Winchell's being admitted to the exclusive clubs that she patronizes in New York.

"I want you to notice," Lockridge quotes her as saying, "that they (the night clubs) have not yet refused entry to that contemptible little reptile who has been slandering us from pillar to post from every gossip-column in the United States."

She also makes a reference to Winchell as "that diseased squirrel."

Winchell thereupon referred to the Duke in his column as "Tweedy-Pie."

The Windsor feuding was mild, compared to the other feuding and fighting which took place in the mid-forties and which was destined to take place in the early fifties.

But it was typical of the people he wrote about that if they failed to live up to what he said about them in his column, he would be perplexed, could become angry to the point of verbal violence.

The strength of a Winchell blast was tremendous.

For fifteen years, when Winchell put someone on his "drop dead" list, they were often better off dead.

He is credited with defeating Congressmen at the polls, with causing Broadway plays to close up and forcing their producers into other fields of endeavor, with destroying the careers of would-be actresses, with driving newspapermen to becoming watch-repair mechanics and oil prospectors, and with juggling and reversing the decisions of motion picture moguls, politicians, and performers about the things they would say and the things they would do.

Long before the age of the red-hunt, Winchell made guilt by association a crime.

Woe unto the producer who would hire an actress Winchell disliked. Woe unto the District Attorney who would continue to employ an assistant with whom Winchell had become vexed.

Winchell had only to slap down those he disliked.

His real power (the broadcast and the column) combined with his mythical power (the mobs, the other important people he knew) made him a figure few men wished to tussle with.

A swank party took place in the mid-forties which was attended by a large number of "top" people in their respective fields.

Playwrights mingled with press agents. Models mixed with hotel-chain owners. Artists jostled with aviation czars.

As was not unusual during those years among that set of people, Winchell's name was mentioned.

The noise quieted as people gathered in a ring and one by one voiced their feelings about the number one columnist.

The sentiments became repetitious. When it seemed that everyone had run out of obscene jokes and flip quips about Winchell, a film producer noticed a model studying her fingernails, apparently bored with the entire discussion.

The producer spoke up. "I'll bet I know someone who has nothing against Winchell," he said. "Gloria over there hasn't even been mentioned. She's probably still hoping."

"Maybe she likes Winchell," somebody else volunteered. "Maybe she likes him because he hasn't mentioned her."

"Oh Winchell, Winchell, Winchell," she said. "Will somebody tell me why everybody dislikes him? It seems so redundant."

23

Private Lives

Mark Hellinger once explained why he didn't become a Winchell competitor.

I wrote scandal once. About ten years ago I think it was. I poured it out in a vitriolic way that only youth and inexperience can produce. I knew that I was hurting people who were defenseless and without a method of retaliation. But I was very young. I kidded myself into believing that this wasn't gossip. No, by God, this was news!

Then, one morning, I broke a story about one of America's greatest comedians in those days. The story was true and I suppose its publication in big headlines was quite justified. But had my outlook then been my outlook of today, I would have tossed the yarn aside and forgotten it.

The comedian's home went to smash after that story, and so did the comedian. The story spelled circulation so we hounded the man until we drove him out of America.

Eventually the comedian came back—a mumbling idiot. I went down to the bay to meet him in order to do a funny story. But when I saw and spoke to him, I came back to the office nauseated.

Since that day, I have never written a line of scandal about anyone. I don't blame the boys who do, because that's what the public wants at all times. But Death itself couldn't force me to do it again. Because, now, I understand.

Fortunately for Hellinger, he didn't have to resort to gossip.

He became a five and ten cent store O. Henry, content to limit his speculations about people to fact and his fantasy to fictitious names.

Once, as a gag, Hellinger wrote an imitation Winchell column. He drew a list of numerous Winchell enemies and wrote nasty innuendoes about them. He drew a list of Winchell's press agent menage and wrote plugs for their clients. He drew a list of national and international celebrities and wrote make-believe gossip about them.

The column was intended as satire but it read very much like a genuine Winchell. It was shown around to friends, but was never published.

There were other gags at Winchell's expense. After Winchell had founded his Damon Runyon Cancer Fund, Ernest Hemingway promised Hellinger that if he died, Hemingway would found the Mark Hellinger Syphilis Fund, with free penicillin for every woman in America.

Hellinger always made a conscious effort to sound hard-boiled and disillusioned.

With Winchell, the hard-boiled bitterness came naturally. Winchell was always of the feeling that people were not showing him enough respect. That he was being short-changed when it came to real affection. That instead of people respecting him for the royalty he felt he was, they were interested only in getting him to put a good word in the column for them and keep the bad words out.

His gruffness and sarcasm were defensive armor.

It is of much consequence that he was obsessed with the fear that he would topple from his place. He was tortured with the fear that the people he thought important wouldn't feel he was important.

The most revealing insight into his lack of genuine

confidence was in the fact that he never dealt directly with the people he was writing about unless they came to him.

He depended on the press agents to tell him about the doings of the "greats" . . . and would never think of calling one of the "greats" directly to get news or check a rumor. There would have been too much possibility of rebuff—of a curt word flung at him or a telephone banged on to its receiver.

He was even hesitant about calling newspapermen he knew well, for fear that they would make sarcastic jibes.

The public was made aware of this peculiar shyness when he wrote that Westbrook Pegler and his wife had moved to a hotel from their home in the country because Pegler was afraid of being kidnapped or beaten.

Pegler was vehement in his denials. It was a typical Winchell lie, he said. If the buffoon of Broadway would have spent thirty-five cents including tax to call Pegler, he could have learned easily and promptly that it was a lie. But Winchell, said Pegler, was a congenital liar, and thrived on lies. He was a gent's room journalist who bathed in the urine left by the wrong-guessers.

However, in time, many of the people he wrote about stopped being angry at the inaccuracies. It wasn't *what* he wrote so much as the effect, intended and real, of what he wrote.

Hellinger had lacked the ability to scrounge around the sewers and make public what he picked up. With Winchell, it was a natural talent. He was without any sense of guilt for the lives he disrupted and the reputations he ruined.

When caught in error, he instinctively became angry at the person about whom he'd written falsely. There was nothing softhearted about him.

That he could rise as he had risen was due to a combination of circumstances, not the least of which was his own lack of taste and his total nonchalance about accuracy.

In the night club zoo, the big monkey was Winchell. At the Stork Club, he was consulted on policy matters. He ordered waiters around as though he were their boss. He fired waiters without consulting the management— and the waiters stayed fired. At the Stork Club, Winchell's word was the law.

On a warm night in September, 1950, the King of the Columnists sat at his table pulling a slice of bread to pieces. He would tear a small chunk of the bread, roll it into a spitball-sized piece, and drop it onto the floor.

The waiter would dutifully pick up the piece of bread.

Winchell would do the same thing with another.

This continued for all of fifteen or twenty minutes. Each time Winchell would drop a glob of bread onto the floor, the waiter would bow, bend, then pick it up.

When Winchell tired of this wordless game, he asked the waiter, "How's your back?"

"Fine, sir," said the waiter.

"That's good," said Winchell. And the game was ended.

People at other tables had been watching with mixed emotions.

"Look somewhere else," he said suddenly in a loud voice. "Or I'll have you all thrown the hell out of here."

The guests in the room looked somewhere else. One of them said reverently, "He's a big man, a very big man. Smart as a whip too. Why do you know he gets a hundred thousand dollars a year for his column, and he doesn't even write it anymore?"

Winchell's camp-followers had become as cockeyed in their perspective of Winchell as he had always been about Winchell's perspective of Winchell.

The gay well-to-do people who flocked to the Stork Club considered it smart to hobnob with infamy.

The radio broadcast differed from the column. As he grew older, Winchell's radio voice sounded less like a garble of Portuguese. But he always had the wisdom not to use any of his international news in the columns, where in the cold light of reason people could analyze it.

He relied almost completely on the International News Service for his international news.

There were few Sunday afternoon papers, and so, much of what he was reporting was new to the listeners.

The mixture was always incredible.

A "flash" about a birth would be followed by "news" that fourteen thousand North Koreans had perished of dysentery that morning would be followed by a plug for a new film would be followed by the information that the President of the United States had a head cold would be followed by the news that two ships had collided in the North Atlantic and all passengers were safe though a crew of fourteen were still floundering in the water would be followed by a commercial for a hand lotion or an automobile or a home permanent or a wrist watch.

"Monday morning papers will confirm," he would shout on an important story, and indeed they would, for the news had been going out over the wire all day. And many of Winchell's listeners believed with honesty and devotion that the Monday morning papers were confirming a Winchell scoop.

Thus, much on the Winchell broadcast was new to the listener—who didn't know that Winchell was saying something that every news editor in the country had on his news spike for hours.

Responsible newscasters considered the Winchell broadcast a hoax.

Boake Carter once remarked that the Winchell program was "a freak that would better belong in a circus side show."

(Winchell had attacked Carter as being "anti-Semitic" during the very weeks when Carter was, unknown to Winchell, training for conversion to the Hebrew faith.)

Actually, his radio scoops wouldn't fill a thimble.

To satisfy the myth that he went one better than the

daily press, Winchell added gossipy "treatment" to the dispatches from the International News Service wire that he used for his Sunday night broadcast.

One result was that he made trivial events sound momentous.

The second result was of considerable amusement to people in the newspaper business.

Winchell would twist the INS news reports into such strange new things that frequently an INS bureau would wire the home office for further information on a story that "Winchell broke tonight on the air."

On checking, it would be discovered that the story went over the INS wire itself—hours before the Winchell broadcast—but that Winchell's treatment had carved it beyond recognition even by the editors who had handled the original dispatch!

Press agents who accompanied him to broadcasts time and again continued to be amused by the little drama that took place each week.

Winchell would broadcast with his hat on and his fly opened.

Vanity had caused him to have his clothes made so tight that he unzipped his pants before each broadcast. He once admitted to a friend that he was "always a little worried" that he might some night forget to zip up his pants again after a broadcast.

The unzipped pants were one reason no women were permitted to witness a broadcast. Later, when he went on television, his concession to the women of America was to wear larger trousers.

His hunger for acclaim was still sharp.

After each broadcast, Winchell waited around the studio with marked impatience for at least ten minutes.

"Any calls?" he asked frequently. He seemed anxious for calls—and, as one press agent put it: "You got the feeling when you watched him that he expected President Roosevelt or Prime Minister Churchill to call him up right after the show."

Finally, he would leave the studio after muttering, "Well, it was a lousy broadcast anyway. I guess nobody listened tonight."

However within a decade he had risen from the eighth most listened to nighttime show, with an estimated 23,000,000 listeners, to the most listened to show with 28,000,000.

He had gradually convinced his listeners that he was on their side. He was, as one writer then described him, "the promise of American freedom and uninhibited bounce; he was Americanism symbolized in a nose-thumbing at the portentousness of the great; he released his listeners for fifteen minutes once a week from the fear of oppression: he was the defender of the American faith."

His second sponsor, the Andrew Jergens Company, found that it was selling lotion with him. He flattered Jergens, praised him, and humbled himself before the greatness of the weekly pay check—which soon exceeded $4,000 a week.

In time, Jergens became one of Winchell's bitterest enemies and tried to harm the columnist by feeding another then-enemy, Westbrook Pegler, with uncomplimentary information about the broadcaster.

But Winchell fed the Winchell myth. And it was still possible to read the most interesting (if untrue) versions of who was sleeping with whom in the daily column, and to hear the bigshots scorned and burned on the radio program.

He had risen as high as he could ever rise.

He had never learned to write a newspaper lead. He had never been able to write a full column on one subject. (The full columns were ghostwritten by press agents and their aides. To make sure that the ghosts wouldn't haunt him by absenting themselves, he also employed a full-time full-length column ghostwriter named Herman Klurfeld, of Bayside, New York.)

He had done as well as any human could ever hope to

do in weaving a tissue of rumor, speculation, plugs, gags and stale news into short, snappy items for people with short snappy taste.

"For an old hoofer, I'm not doing badly," he once said. And for an old hoofer, he wasn't.

24

The Political Winchell

Walter Winchell's entrance into the political arena was to have the most marked effects upon his public life.

In his early days the columnist showed no inclination to get mixed up in politics. In his later days, he showed no understanding of them. Yet it has been politics which drew Winchell into his greatest blunders, and his incredible innocence of them which led to his peak as a power, and then to his sharp decline.

The political beginnings were gentle. In the rat-tat-tat of his radio pitch, he would insert items about politicians and their intentions. This carried over into the columns.

"Another political expose' will soon explode in Brooklyn," he wrote. Nothing much happened in Brooklyn that year except the Dodgers.

Two weeks before Franklin Roosevelt publicly announced that he would run for a third term, Winchell stated flatly:

FDR will announce that he isn't going to seek a third term any day now.

Winchell played it safe for the third term election and the day before the election he didn't have a word to say for or against either candidate.

But he made no secret of the fact that he was, at heart,

a Roosevelt man. Critics said that the columnist was FDR-inclined because he wanted to be "popular" and "run with the pack."

It is true that election returns showed his politics were popular with the general populace. Nevertheless Winchell's pro-Roosevelt sentiment wasn't "popular" with his boss, William Randolph Hearst. Nor was it popular with the newspapers which published his syndicated column. Eighty to ninety percent of the nation's newspapers opposed Roosevelt by 1940. Winchell's column appeared almost exclusively in this eighty to ninety percent group.

Some newspapers censored the Winchell column. Others dropped it entirely. Nevertheless he stuck to his guns, and in fact imported larger cannon.

It was not only the flattery that Roosevelt had blown his way, but his mounting obsession about Hitler.

Hitler had made Winchell conscious of his Jewishness. Winchell became a merciless scavenger and denouncer of race hate in low places and high places. After Hitler invaded Russia, Winchell was given added encouragement in his anti-Hitler crusade by a clique of Communists who were at that time in high places in the Anti-Defamation League and also by Abraham Fastenberg who was assuming the name Arnold Forster and was also trying to assume command of the A.D.L.

Forster provided Winchell with material so the columnist could air attacks against the bigots. Winchell also unwittingly aired Forster's own private feuds.

Winchell quickly divided everyone into good guys or bad guys. Certain Congressmen were good guys. Others were bad guys.

It wasn't always easy on his readers.

Being pro-Winchell meant being inconsistent. It meant supporting those people and things who seemed to support Winchell, and attacking those people and things who didn't.

On his broadcast, Winchell referred to the voters who had supported isolationist Congressmen in the 1940 election as "those damn fools who reelected them."

So many thousands of protest poured into the network over his use of "damn" on the Sabbath, that both the network and Winchell were forced to make a contrite apology on the following week's broadcast.

"Dear Mr. Winchell," a reader wrote, "You've got me puzzled. Today you attack Communists but yesterday you ran a complete column by a woman who has identified herself as a Communist, and who is openly living with a writer who has identified himself as a Communist."

Winchell's reply?

"I don't pry into the conjugal affairs of other people," he wrote.

(This was a safe answer since Winchell's girl friend of the moment was also known to be a Communist.)

But if his political sights were muddied, he felt that he knew the enemy. He fought anti-Semitism and anti-Negroism and Fascism in all its native forms.

He wrote about the bigotry and racial discrimination that others only dared whisper about. He named names.

He singled out Congressmen like Representatives Dies, Rankin and Hoffman and he went into a frenzy of indignation about their activities.

It was perhaps poetic justice that Winchell, who built the little lie into a national industry should work to alert America to Hitler who had parlayed the big lie into an empire.

Once a week, on his Sunday night broadcast, he gave reassurance to his audience of twenty million people that its fear of the Nazi oppressors could be overcome by confidence in democracy.

Motivations aside, it was this period in Winchell's life which lifted him from the gossip columnist circle into a statue-sized national idol.

Medals were heaped upon him. Awards came at a rate that made new ones anticlimactical.

When Forster had first advised him to "become active in domestic and world politics" he had replied that it "isn't my racket."

But other advisors among his press agent claque told him: "With your acting talents, they'll never get wise. Go ahead and fake it."

A New Jersey newspaper editor, H. B. Haines, had warned: "Crusading is a rich man's game. You lose advertising, you lose circulation, you even lose prestige. People begin to think you have a personal axe to grind and that you're working for some ulterior motive. And even when you have thwarted the plans of scheming politicians and have saved the city . . . what happens? No one gives a damn!"

Winchell ground his axe and rather than lose prestige, he gained it; rather than lose circulation, he gained it.

The menace of Hitlerism was real enough. The menace of Fascism was real enough. Winchell was not the only one who now took Winchell seriously.

He wrote of himself in *Coronet:* "There is no liberal advance in the last thirty years that this reporter hasn't supported."

"He's a regular jock strap," quipped Congressman Martin Dies.

Winchell's number one ghost, Irving Hoffman, told Winchell, "A liberal is a fellow who has both feet firmly planted in the air."

Winchell liked that and printed it.

Usually however, his approach to the world situation was too intense to allow for jesting.

"Winchell is trying to lead this country into a war," warned the America First Committee.

He didn't have to test his leadership qualities fully, for on December 7, 1941, the Japanese attacked Pearl Harbor.

Winchell went into the Navy as a Lieutenant Commander. He manned table 50 at the Stork Club in his full uniform.

"Winchell is making the highest sacrifice for the war effort," one of his critics wrote. "He is giving up olives in his martinis for the duration."

Cissie Patterson, whose Washington Times-Herald carried the Winchell column, killed all but nine of twenty-eight columns in one month.

According to a Washington story, she was telling people: "There isn't a night goes by that I don't get down on my knees and pray that they take the bastard off shore duty and put him on a destroyer that will sink."

But the columnist concentrated his fire on the higher echelons.

"Hitler is losing on the ground in Russia, in the air over Germany and on the sands of Africa. He seems to win only in Congress," he wrote.

And: "Congress includes some of the sorriest stumblebums in the Nation."

And: "What are the saboteurs doing in Congress? Why doesn't Congress clean its own house."

Winchell wanted a lot of housecleaning. In one column he wrote: "You can say of any one of 435 Congressmen, 'He'll go down in history as the Louse of Representatives.'"

He called Congress "The Monkey House" and "The Washington Rogues Gallery."

It was inevitable that some of the Congressmen he was attacking would strike back.

On April 3, 1944, *The New Republic* declared:

"Probably no individual in the United States . . . now has a more widespread and better deserved reputation for exposing really subversive activities than Mr. Winchell.

"Again and again, on the radio and in his signed column, he has called attention to persons who in this country were doing the work of Goebbels, or were his native counterpart . . .

"Mr. Martin Dies is now occupied in trying to embarrass Mr. Winchell by all the methods in his arsenal. To subpoena all the records and papers of a busy journalist for two years is by itself no mean punishment."

"The Truth can be wounded—but it always lives to win the fight," Winchell screamed.

25

Quagmire

In 1953, during the course of a pre-trial examination in one of the many libel suits brought against him, Walter Winchell was asked certain questions about his political affiliations.

His responses which were frank and apparently sincere, were surprising admissions for the Winchell he had become.

WINCHELL ADMITS
REDS 'USED' HIM

was the headline in the *Herald-Tribune* report on the examination.

The *New York Times* headlined it:

POSSIBLE RED DUPE,
WINCHELL ADMITS

In the examination, the columnist confessed to all his past "errors." He admitted that he had plugged "Plot Against The Peace" until it became a best-selling book. The book was written by two gentlemen named Sayers and Khan.

"They turned out to be Communists," Winchell said. Then, without being asked, he added: "Incidentally, I plugged another book called 'Secret Armies' which exposed the Joe McWilliamses and all the other people we were fighting and this fellow (who wrote the book) turned out to be a Communist."

Among the spectators at the examination were William Conklin of the *New York Times* (which paper Winchell had falsely accused of harboring 100 dues paying Communists); Erwin Knoll of *Editor & Publisher* (whose late editor, Marlen Pew, once battled Winchell in an incident described earlier in this book); Myron Kauffman of Associated Press (which association Winchell had falsely accused of "stealing" his "scoops"); and Alvin Davis, L. H. Cook, and George Trow of the *New York Post* (which paper Winchell had falsely accused of harboring a nest of subversives).

It wasn't exactly a squad of well-wishers.

They sat quietly and listened, perhaps with some satisfaction, as attorneys read portions of old Winchell columns to the columnist.

The portions dealt with Russia, with Stalin, with Communism.

Once, when an attorney began to read a column from 1945 titled "Things I Never Knew Till Now—about Russia," Winchell asked, "Can I look? It might be usable again."

"Well, I'll show you one that you might not like to publish again," the attorney said. "This one says: 'The Russians were very generous in handling the Polish werewolves in the Moscow trials . . .' That is dated June 28, 1945. You wouldn't want to republish that today, would you?"

"I might," Winchell replied.

"And do you now believe that the Russians were 'very generous' in the Moscow trials?" the lawyer demanded.

"I believed it then. I have had no information on it since then."

Later, the attorney read another portion of a column. "You wrote, 'Insiders tell you that Stalin in his grab for

Poland, didn't confiscate an inch of territory belonging to the Catholic Church.'"

"Insiders tell you . . ." Winchell remarked.

"You wanted the outsiders to know it?"

"It was news as I got it," Winchell said.

"Just answer my question."

"That apparently was the news as I found it at the time. I found that to be news that perhaps nobody else got and I thought I had it alone."

Item after item was read to the columnist, who was forced to sit squirming in his chair.

The first examination took two and a half hours. A week later, a second examination took more than four hours.

While Winchell tried to be a hale-fellow-well-met during his first examination, he was nervous and irritable at the second meeting.

"I thought the old boy would blow his top any minute," one of the spectators later remarked.

It was during the second examination that pages and pages of pro-Communist material written by Walter Winchell was flung back at Walter Winchell.

He had called Whittaker Chambers "The Marx of Time." He had praised Communist authors, Communist-line plays, Stalin, Lenin, and Russia.

Winchell pressed his lips together in anger as some of the material was read into the record. He snorted at other items. Occasionally he tried to defend his ancient columns. When questioned about his praise for Communist author Howard Fast, Winchell declared: "I still think he is very good. In fact, we have an awful lot of writers, very fine writers . . ." His voice trailed off into a mumble.

At another point he claimed that when he plugged a book by a Communist Party-affiliated publishing house, he was unaware of the affiliation. Under questioning, he admitted: "I may have plugged a book even after I found out about it. I don't know."

The attorney who was questioning him was patient and courteous. In a soft voice he asked, "Mr. Winchell, you wouldn't like someone to confront you with something you wrote eight years ago and to be held up to public scorn because it happened to be wrong?"

"It has been done," Winchell said, a little sadly.

"You didn't like it?"

"I didn't say I liked it, but I didn't sue anybody about it."

The attorney smiled. It was shortly thereafter that he gained the admission from Winchell which made the *Times* and *Tribune* headlines.

In answer to the question: "Do you think you have been used by the Communists?" he replied, "I would say yes."

"And was your column used as a place to plant pro-Communist propaganda?"

"I'm wide open to that," Winchell said. "Anyone is who writes for publication."

It was a far different Winchell who spoke that day than the Winchell of ten years before.

The Walter Winchell of 1941-2-3-4-5 was a firebrand. If he traced the struggle for free speech back to Patrick Henry's fight with "George V" (instead of George III) he could be forgiven. His point was the important thing.

If he wrote that twenty-two persons, many of them "high Government officials" had been trapped by the FBI in a plot to spread false news in wartime, he could be forgiven. His theme was patriotism. (The FBI denied all knowledge of the coup. Army Intelligence told a *Herald-Tribune* reporter: "Since Mr. Winchell is a Commodore of some sort, you'd better contact the Navy." The Navy denied all knowledge of the story. . . .)

He was eternally vigilant.

He pursued Dies and Rankin and Hoffman and they pursued him. He pursued Gerald L. K. Smith and Gerald Winrod and Colonel Lindbergh and John T. Flynn and Elizabeth Dilling and Joseph Kamp.

He went after the isolationists and the Roosevelt critics and the Negro-baiters and the anti-Semites and the military pessimists—lumping them together as if they were all one thing.

He "knocked off" politicians in the same the-hell-with-ethics-or-truth way in which he'd trained himself to knock off all Winchell critics and Winchell "enemies."

For instance, unable to secure any other disparaging information about a Congressman he disliked, he wrote:

When Congressman Lambertson was at the White House recently, Mrs. Roosevelt probably asked him to put his shoes on. That dimwit misrepresentative used to walk through his home town streets barefoot with trousers rolled to the knees.

In 1943, the Winchell column contained this item of advice and information:

. . . the Nazis called every anti-Nazi a Communist. Now the new scare word in America comes clear. Think not that it means you are a Communist. It may mean only he doesn't like you. It may mean only that he who calls you a Communist is himself a Fascist. Such is the Nazi technique in America as in Germany now . . .

(Years later, through innuendo and by tight-rope walking over the libel net, he was to use the Communist smear against his enemies. It didn't mean that they were Communists. It meant only that Winchell didn't like them.)

A resolution introduced in the House of Representatives in 1943 asked why Winchell, then a Naval Reserve officer on "active duty" had not been punished for some of the things he was saying over the radio and in his columns. He was violating naval law by criticizing politicians publicly.

A few weeks later it was announced that Winchell had been placed on inactive duty. There was no elaboration of this bare announcement.

Winchell complained to his press agents: "They didn't want me in Samoa, they wanted me off the radio."

And indeed, some people did want him off radio. He

had offended Catholics by writing about Joan of Arc as "too sexy to wear dresses" and by repeating an untrue smear about a prominent Catholic layman, Senator David I. Walsh.

On June 28, 1942, the Knights of Columbus passed a resolution calling on the Federal Communications Commission to withdraw broadcasting facilities from Winchell.

He told a *Newsweek* reporter, in commenting on his military trouble, "My fangs have been removed and my typewriter fingers are being rapped with the butt of a gun."

But now the Dies-Winchell battle was to become even hotter.

Winchell spewed so much vitriolic scorn on his radio broadcast that Representative Dies demanded and received Winchell's fifteen minutes on Sunday to make a statement. Winchell was given the 9:15 to 9:30 spot to reply to Dies.

Dies, without mentioning the organization by name, leveled his attack on the Anti-Defamation League. He said that Winchell was being "used" by "one of the most sinister forces this nation ever faced." The force, said Dies, "is a highly organized and well-financed enterprise to destroy by vilification the character of any public man who gets in the way."

(By a quirk of circumstance, the Anti-Defamation League ten years later did become "a well-financed enterprise which tried to destroy by vilification the character of public men who got in its way." But in those days the only legitimate criticism which could be leveled at it was that it employed too many Communists, and that they were hampering its efforts at being a pro-democratic enemy of bigotry.)

The Dies broadcast and Winchell rejoinder took place on the night of March 26, 1943. Pollsters indicate that never before or since did the Winchell program have so great a listening audience.

After Dies spoke, Winchell came on. His voice was charged with an emotional mixture of fear and anger. Twice his voice cracked as he struggled with a script which was obviously inadequate for the occasion.

Press photographers insisted that the two men pose in a handclasp. Winchell was so upset that the picture had to be held up until he could muster control of his shaking hand.

Dies had been a young comer in Congress. He had set the pace for future un-American Activities Committees. He was a Democrat from an uncontested Democratic area of Texas.

The full story of the pressures, threats and frameup (which took place in a Los Angeles hotel) has never been told. A few weeks later, Dies announced that he would not seek re-election. He offered no reason for his decision, but the announcement was obviously one of personal defeat.

On May 15, 1944, Winchell boasted in his column:

Sudden thawt: Martin Dies quit because there were two obstacles he couldn't overcome. Winchell's opposition and Pegler's support.

In reporting on his victory, Winchell quoted from the *Richmond Times Dispatch.* As might be expected, he quoted only those sections which made Winchell look pretty good and Dies look pretty bad.

"The impending retirement of Representative Martin Dies from the House is certainly no cause for grief. Dies' Committee on Un-American Activities has done some good work in uncovering subversive elements in the government, but for every bona fide Communist or fellow traveler thus unveiled, he has smeared a dozen, if not a hundred innocent persons.

"A typical example of Dies technique was his charge in 1942 that 1121 persons in the Federal service were guilty of subversive activity. The FBI accordingly spent $100,000 investigating half those on the list . . . Two

dismissals and one disciplinary action were the total results."

Winchell would have a further near-encounter with
Dies in ten years. By that time he had made the full circle, and was scheduled to attend a dinner in honor of
J. B. Matthews. Matthews, working with Dies, had mas-
ter-minded the assault on Winchell.

Both Winchell and Dies were scheduled to attend the
dinner. Present too would be some of the race-hate sales-
men Winchell used to attack, including Merwin K. Hart,
Allen Zoll and Joseph Kamp.

But the embarrassment of Winchell and Dies facing
each other was too much for both men. Dies sent a telegram of apology and Winchell telephoned his personal
regrets to Matthews.

Each believed the other would attend. And so neither
attended.

It was during the early forties that Winchell became
obsessed with the idea that America had fallen into the
grip of a press monopoly which would only tell one side
of the political story. The side Winchell didn't agree
with.

The Hearst papers had omitted an entire column some
years before. It was a guest column in which playwright
Lillian Hellman gave a first-hand account of the bomb-
ing of civilians in Madrid by the Spanish Fascists.

Winchell was bitter about being suppressed.

Until that time, some papers had cut small parts of his
column because of space limitations. If he didn't approve
of the way they did this, he would order his syndicate
to drop that paper from the Winchell list when its contract was up for renewal. Otherwise he had experienced
little trouble with censorship.

He'd been permitted to say anything he pleased. He'd
been allowed to make gross errors, and to refuse to correct them.

But suddenly the Hearst syndicate began to cut whole

chunks from his column. These were mostly low-blow attacks on Wendell Wilkie.

Winchell harangued anger and grief at all who would listen. The outcome was that arrangements were made in secret for him to use the censored column material in a separate column to be published in the newspaper PM.

That left-wing New York daily was hitting its stride. It was attacking the people Winchell was attacking and exposing some of the bigots and race-hate merchants who were attacking Winchell. It was a natural all around.

Because of his commitments to Hearst, Winchell was not allowed to write a column for any paper outside of the Hearst King Features orbit.

So he gave full rein to his sentiments under a pseudonym.

Years later, when he thought the few people who'd known had forgotten his extra-curricular chore or would be "gentlemen enough to keep quiet," Winchell attacked PM. Although there were no more than a handful of Communists among many hundreds of employees (including an heir to the Great Atlantic & Pacific Tea Company), Winchell said the paper was staffed "mostly by Communists."

The name he signed to his columns for PM was "Paul Revere II."

Gradually, he drifted to the right.

His attitudes were often mixed on other matters but they were consistent in the matter of unions. He was against them.

His newspaper career had begun on an anti-union paper, and the attitude stuck.

When he resigned from the American Newspaper Guild he wrote that he was quitting their "club."

"The least the bastard could have said," a union official complained, "was that he was resigning from a union, not a club."

But Winchell's scorn for the union movement almost equalled that of his one-time enemy, Westbrook Pegler.

For example, during the depression, cafe entertainers formed the American Federation of Actors (AFL), affiliated with Actors Equity.

One day a press agent told Winchell that the AFA was forcing chorus girls to pay dues but that the union wasn't giving them any protection.

Winchell never bothered to check the complaint, though the union's headquarters were conveniently located at the Hotel Edison, and the union was headed by Sophie Tucker.

Instead, his column carried a violent anti-AFA blast, which hurt the union's prestige and made it more difficult for it to police the cafes.

Ralph Whitehead who was executive secretary of the union, tried without success to contact Winchell.

Discovering at last that the Stork Club was the only place where Winchell could be seen, he went to the Stork. There he met Winchell and pleaded with him to retract the false statement.

One day later, Winchell blasted the union again, this time calling Whitehead "blockhead" and "blackhead."

Whitehead subsequently had a nervous collapse. The union folded. Later, it was succeeded by AGVA.

One year after World War II ended, he was crying for war with Russia.

The *Cincinnati Enquirer,* which carried his column, became fed up with what it called his "flap-jawed" talk. In an editorial in February 1948, it warned its readers that Winchell didn't know what he was talking about.

Said the newspaper: "Walter Winchell has had us on the very verge of war with Russia almost every Sunday night for the last two years with his constant poisoning of public opinion. How has transom-peeker Winchell become an expert in foreign affairs? He has trained for it on items about who is going to get divorced, and who is going to have a baby and approximately when."

On January 27, 1946, Winchell also entered the scientific world when he announced this heretofore and since unknown news:

Uranium is now obsolete in the production of atomic bombs . . . Lead works just as well.

Where the Roosevelt Administration pampered Winchell, the Truman Administration loathed him.

His ego pricked, he tried to loathe back. More and more he was forced into the camp of the extreme right-wing Republicans. The same race-baiters he had once attacked now fed him material.

Amusingly enough, the Communist-liners were also able to snuggle even closer to him. One press agent who had worked diligently to elect Communist candidates to the New York City counsel, now fed Winchell make-believe items "against" Communists. These always skirted actual Communists and damaged their arch-enemies, the liberals.

The press agent continues to feed Winchell today and has boasted that "Walter is in my pocket."

Someone persuaded Winchell to oppose a unified military command. Winchell began to call proponents of such a command "traitors."

He said a unified command would be "the last will and testament of the American republic."

The military command has been unified and the republic is still breathing.

In the "War We Do Not Want" issue of *Colliers* published on October 27, 1951, Winchell contributed a column headed "Walter Winchell In Moscow," indicating that he intended to be among the first tourists after *Colliers'* invasion of Russia. He chided the Russian people for not having taken the United Nations more seriously.

Meanwhile he tried desperately to keep pace with the professional anti-Communists and to prove that he was a 100 percent loyal American. It was a near hysterical attempt to erase the past, which threatened to catch up with him with every session of the Congressional investigating committees.

When word reached Winchell that Senator McCarthy would level his next headline hunt against Winchell, the columnist quaked.

His fear was so apparent that a Stork Club associate remarked in apparent surprise, "Mr. W. acts like he has a yellow streak down his back as big as his column."

McCarthy told friends that Winchell pleaded with him to "lay off." The Senator proudly explained that Winchell swore he would never say another unpleasant thing about McCarthy; that he would cooperate whenever possible.

McCarthy never said an unkind thing about Winchell and on one occasion had a Winchell column reprinted in the Congressional Record.

All of this happened a few weeks after McCarthy had attacked Drew Pearson. The Senator had been tipped that Adams Hats was dropping the Pearson show anyway. Other sponsors were waiting in line to sponsor Pearson.

What happened is that the McCarthy blast frightened other sponsors away.

Instead of coming to the defense of his radio colleague (the two men had often cooperated before), Winchell played it safe. He stayed mum.

Since then McCarthy has fed items to Winchell which Winchell has dutifully used.

Winchell does everything possible to endear himself to the Senator. He has plugged McCarthy's favorite reading matter, a publication called *Counterattack*.

It is filled with almost as many errors of fact as Winchell's own column.

26

Private Women

Winchell's moral code has always been a personal thing.

In the roaring twenties, Florenz Ziegfeld used to warn his show girls against dating Broadway columnists, but especially Winchell.

"He has the worst reputation on Broadway where women are concerned," Ziegfeld said frequently. "Any girl who wants to remain proper will not date Winchell."

Wilson Mizner put it differently. "There are two ways for a show girl to become famous. Vertically and horizontally. If you're going to do it horizontally, it will be quicker if you know Winchell."

In the little world of Walter Winchell, vulgarity was disguised as sophistication. Much of the night club after hours talk turned on who was outsmarting whom by sleeping with whose wife, fiancee or husband.

Sexual conquests were casual, usually were local night club knowledge, and frequently were business deals on a strict "If I do this for you what will you do for me" level.

When he was too young to be cautious, Winchell would parade his women where they could be seen and admired. Each new woman was a sop to his nervous insecurity about his place in society and the world.

Like an adolescent showing off, he would kiss and paw his companion of the evening for all to see. Once he pretended to get into an argument about the size of his then-current girl's bust measurement. He insisted that the waiter find a tape measure, and then he blandly measured her bust from all angles, taking other steps to assure all watchers that she wasn't wearing falsies.

Early in their marriage, when June Winchell refused to appear publicly with him anymore, Winchell made a short-lived effort to "reform."

At that time Mark Hellinger told Winchell, "A married man can't be running around too much, Walter. At least, not running where so many people can see him."

However pretty women provided ego gratification too necessary to his makeup to be given up.

When he rented a top-floor suite at the St. Moritz Hotel on Central Park South, he would escort his lady friends through the lobby in the early morning hours, and send them home alone around noon of the next day.

A combination of circumstances caused him to change his ways. Among the wrong rumors he heard was that "the mob" would try to blackmail him after framing him with a youngster who was below the age of consent.

Another factor that brought on caution was his knowledge that he was making many enemies, and that some of them might be imaginative enough to hire private investigators to chronicle his romantic doings.

But the incident that made an indelible impression on him happened to a friend. The friend, a newspaperman with Hearst, was married too. Unlike Winchell, he had no extra girl friend, but like Winchell, he had made enemies.

One night, the friend's wife left their second floor walkup apartment to take in a movie, as was her custom on Monday evenings.

A minute after she'd left, there was a rapping on the door. Thinking his wife had returned for something she'd forgotten, the man swung open the door.

The next scene took place in less time than it takes to describe it. A fifteen year old girl rushed past him, ripped off her blouse and brassiere, and screamed "Help! Police!"

With the first cry, two policemen came running up the stairs, their pistols drawn.

"This man tried to rape me!" the girl sobbed.

The man was given a choice of facing charges for attempted rape of a minor, or of leaving town within twenty-four hours.

After making a desperate round of his friends, including Winchell, he left town with his wife, never to return to New York City.

Winchell was shocked. He had called the Police Commissioner and had been told to "lay off." He had gone to Hearst executives and they had shrugged their shoulders helplessly.

People he knew on the police force and in gangland circles, assured him that it was much easier for a man to defend himself on a crime he had committed than on one where he was framed and was innocent.

(In a way, the people Winchell hurt through his column had learned this. The less truth there was to his innuendo, the more difficult it was to persuade people it wasn't true.)

From then on, Winchell exercised restraint both in his choice of women and in his love-making habits with them.

He would have a girl rent a private apartment, only to abandon it (and her) after a month or two. Or he would sneak them into the St. Moritz by entering quietly through the servants' entrance on Fifty-Eighth Street.

He was always fearful of being photographed in the act of bringing a woman into his hotel. His fears went unrealized.

Love came to Walter Winchell in the shape of a tall show girl from Texas who possessed tremendous charm and poise. Her name was Mary Lou Bently.

When they met, she was sixteen years old.

According to the experts in those things, she was easily one of the most attractive show girls ever to hit Broadway. She was like a beautiful dream from the distant past, for in the middle of the twentieth century, show girls were more tart than art, their sole task being to parade beneath spotlights in various stages of undress and in various colorful costumes.

But Mary Lou Bently couldn't have looked stupid and clumsy if she'd tried.

The first thing you noticed about her was her walk. She knew how to walk, on stage and off.

It was the walk that first attracted Winchell.

Later, when the couple were going together, Winchell temporarily abandoned his Stork Club table for one at the Versailles where he would say to press agents who were viewing her for the first time, "I don't have to point her out. You'll know her. She stands out from all the others."

With Mary Lou Bently, Winchell once again thrust aside caution. Once again, after a many-year interval, he would walk through the front entrance of the St. Moritz with his female companion; would be seen publicly with her in the clubs.

"It's the first time I've ever really been in love," he told a friend. "I never knew what it was like before. She's wonderful."

It was Mary Lou who insisted on "keeping up appearance" by her officially rooming with Mary Dowell whom Winchell helped make famous as "Stuttering Sam" Dowell, calling her "prettiest of the Texas skyscrapers . . ."

Mary Lou Bently was Winchell's sweetheart during the height of his glory in the early forties. The couple were seen everywhere together—though no columnist dared to "item" that one.

She was as impressed with him as he was with her. As "Winchell's girl" other show girls looked upon her as something special. The owners of the various clubs where she worked treated her with special consideration.

Winchell, always afraid of being "taken" by a woman, spent very little money on her, but Mary Lou had never been accustomed to too much. She was content and he was ecstatic.

Mary Lou Bently was a cluster-symbol to Winchell.

She was his lost youth. She was the gay era of Texas Guinan's that would never be again for him. She was calmness and confidence, beauty and grace. Where he was a minority in a minority in a minority, she sprang from the heart of America and was cool and clean and untarnished by the lust and ambition that still burned deep in the heart of Winchell.

She had no goal beyond feeding and clothing herself and enjoying herself. He had no goal but he knew he must work hard to the last day he lived to retain the illusion of power and importance so dear to him.

And then the flame cooled.

At first it was imperceptible as those things are. Their mutual interest had endured for years. And then, they both discovered their relationship had become a habit. They saw each other less and less.

One night she refused to permit him into her apartment when he'd taken her home.

"What gives? I'm no stage door Johnny."

"It's over, Walter," she said. "You know that."

"There's someone else?"

"Yes."

He turned and left without saying goodnight. For a week he was absent from his usual haunts. Although he had seemed to be willing to relinquish the Bently girl before, the thought of someone else succeeding him was too much to bear.

He flew to Miami. There he cried on Al Jolson's shoulder.

"I don't understand it," he said. "The kid was crazy about me."

Meanwhile, he'd hired a private detective to follow Mary Lou and see who had taken his place.

The man's name was Frank Gallop. He was a radio announcer with a voice so distinguished that General Motors selected him to do all their important radio and television commercials in 1952 and 1953.

A few years after the breakup, Mary Lou Bently was scheduled to work at the Diamond Horseshoe.

Winchell called Billy Rose. "I want you to keep your hands off that girl," he commanded.

"I'm not interested in her," Rose muttered.

"Just the same, I know your reputation. You lay off that girl."

The Gallop affair lasted a few years, then it cooled and the couple parted good friends.

In 1950, Mary Lou married an army officer and at this writing is with him somewhere in Japan.

The unique feeling Winchell had for her may have been indicated by the fact that he showed no column animosity toward Gallop.

Once, when the Winchell show was looking for an announcer, Gallop's name was submitted by his booking agency.

Gallop, on learning this, suggested to the advertising agency handling the Winchell show, that they check with the columnist. Winchell told the agency it was okey with him if Gallop auditioned.

Gallop auditioned with six other announcers. He didn't get the job.

The man who made an industry out of the rumor now became the victim of one himself. "They" were saying that he had become impotent. "They" cited as proof the fact that he had become especially vicious in his attacks on almost anybody who showed an inclination toward healthy sex.

Somewhere along the line, Winchell decided to take himself a new woman.

He had passed the age where a young girl like Mary Lou Bently would take him seriously. It was in 1953 and he had passed his peak.

Jane Kean was part of a sister act which had been around a long time. The sisters first gained some prominence when one of them substituted for Betty Garrett in the Broadway musical review "Call Me Mister" while the other took the same role in the road company of that show.

The sisters were so-so comedians, and the parade seemed to be passing them by.

One of them, Betty, was the mother of a nine year old girl named Deedee sired by actor Frank Faye. She'd lived with him for many years, and then one day she reminded him that he once said he'd marry her.

By this time Fay had gotten religion. He explained that in the eyes of the Catholic church he was still married to Barbara Stanwyck and so couldn't marry again.

It was at this point that the couple parted ways.

Visitors who asked about the little boy were told simply and frankly by the sisters: "That's Faye's kid."

When Winchell became enchanted with the Kean girls, he had a hard time picking sides.

But after some trials and tribulations, he decided that his strongest affection was for Jane.

The friendship gave Winchell a much-needed shot in the arm. And this time he took no chances on coming out of it.

Once before, he had joined a vaudeville actress in her boudoir and her first words after playing footsie with him were: "I want to get paid off in plugs for this, Walter."

This time he was paying off even before he was asked:

Within a two month period he gave the Kean sisters twenty-one full-blown plugs.

To an uninformed observer, it would seem that the

Kean sisters had become the most exciting thing in show business since Rin Tin Tin.

"Every big-time talent agency is vying to sign Betty & Jane Kean, who are killing the people in Vegas at the Sands . . ." he wrote.

"Matty Fox sent those Kean gals a contract which their barristers are studying. 'At least a dozen teevy films' annually for the 'Betty-Jane Kean Corporation.' Two weeks ago (before Orchids here) they were a Sister Act. Now they're gonna be a Corporation! . . ." he wrote.

"Betty and Jane Kean open at Ciro's (Hollywood) Apr. 15th following their Riverside (Reno) booking. Then the London Palladium. At twice the wages of a year ago. The British go maaad over talent . . ." he wrote.

"Betty and Jane Kean fly to the Palladium (London) at sundown tomorrow and most of the girls around midtown are damn glad! (Jeee!)" he wrote.

"Betty & Jane Kean (now in the skies bound for the London Palladium) who left with terrific teevy, radio and recording offers from Manie Sachs at NBC, Bob Kintner at ABC and CBS' Harry Ackerman," he wrote.

"Before flying to the London Palladium Jane and Betty Kean were worried about the reported banana-famine there . . ." he wrote.

His friendship carried him as far as Los Angeles where he spent hours in Jane's Beverly Hills Hotel room. He was a little old to do much of the usual thing so he mostly did what was usual for him: He talked about himself.

He was no longer the "old Winchell" who would slip into hotels through the service entrance, mortally afraid that someone would "get something on him."

By now it had been gotten. Winchell entered hotels by their front entrance.

One morning at three-thirty o'clock the door to Jane's room opened quietly, and Winchell slipped out.

As he did, he came face to face with an old enemy.

The following Sunday he announced on his program:

"To the chief of police: A bookie is in town and if he comes five feet closer to me I'm going to have to protect myself."

Now it is to Winchell's credit that of the many things which were said about him nobody ever said he was psychotic—that he had lost contact with reality.

But a few days later in his column he gave vent to his imaginative wishful thinking. He wrote: "This reporter (last Sunday night) alerted the Bevills police chief (Clinton Anderson) that a procurer (named in the Jelke vice case) was in his rich community 'up to no good' . . . Chief Anderson collared the Broadway 'producer' (whose profiles are in the Rogues' Gallery in N.Y.C.) and told him to get out of town in 5 minutes . . . His companion (featuring a walrus mustache) got hysterical . . . 'I'm a respectable banker on Long Island,' he choked. 'This will ruin me if publicized!' . . . 'It's against the law,' the Chief reminded the sucker, 'to consort with criminals. This man has a long record' . . . We make it public to save the chump (an obvious set-up) from a clipping . . . We are omitting the bank executive's name this time. His last initial is B . . ."

Said Chief of Police Anderson: "I don't know what Winchell is talking about."

Winchell returned to New York, where he continued to give the Kean sisters their plug payoffs.

Others got into the act. A songwriter named Jule Styne announced that he would sign the sister team for a Broadway show he planned to produce.

Said Styne to his press agent: "You know maybe a better way we can be chummy with Winchell?"

The press agent didn't know a better way.

27

Toni

The part of Winchell's personal life that is most often talked about in Broadway circles is the obsession he has about his daughter Walda. In Winchell's eyes, no man is good enough for her and he has gone to unusual lengths to discourage romantic entanglements.

It is almost as if Walter Winchell feels he is competing with his daughter's suitors.

The strain of the strange father-daughter relationship is part of the tale that wags Winchell today.

In his column on October 10, 1934, Winchell made his first public show of affection toward his daughter. It was a gentle expression of fatherly warmth.

I happened to be near 62nd and Central Park West about 4:30 this morning and I saw a fellow try to die. He drank iodine and then fell in the gutter. The cops forced milk down his throat, and he fought them. He didn't want to live. In searching his pockets they found nothing to indicate his name and address. Just a folder with his kid's photo, a little girl, about Walda's age, and a letter in child's writing, it began: "Dear Daddy, I miss you so . . ." His whole story was in that pocketbook, which contained no money. He probably was out of a job, and his wife had left him. There was a piece of legal paper which said the courts had decreed he could see his child once every three months, poor guy.

I guess I'm a lucky man, honey . . . where's Walda?

Walda was then nine years old.

Walda gradually came to look upon her father with some of the loathing of the neglected daughter of an embittered mother.

(Papa had named her Walda but since childhood she had been running away from identification with him. She called herself Eileen and then on entering show business as an actress, she assumed the name Toni Eden. That's the name she uses today. That's the name in the mailbox of her modest midtown Manhattan apartment.)

The atmosphere of the home life of the Winchells was not conducive to happiness for their growing daughter.

Walda, or rather Toni, complained to neighbors that her father would scream and rant at her mother, her brother and herself for hours at a time, often using the vilest gutter language.

As far back as she could remember, her father hated every boy she ever went out with. After a date she would hear the familiar refrain over and over again: "What do they want me to write about them?" and "Don't you know he's going out with you just to get in good with me?"

There was also the familiar threat, "If that bum ever sets foot in this house again I'll fix him and his family. I've got plenty on them," etc., etc.

Toni met her dates elsewhere. No longer did she dare bring a friend to the house.

As she tried to pursue her acting career, she confided to friends that her family life was so unbearable that she would marry the first man that asked her, just to get away from home.

She was encouraged in this attitude by Winchell's lawyer, Ernest Cuneo, who told her, "You'll never be happy until you get out of the house."

She was appearing in a play on Broadway, and met William Lawless, a young interior decorator from Cambridge, Massachusetts. He was still in uniform, having just been discharged from the service.

She met him on June 3. On June 4, the couple went to West New York, New Jersey, and were married.

Winchell learned about the marriage in a competitor's Broadway column.

He was having his usual gay time in the girlie capital, Hollywood. He made a long-distance call to his wife and daughter. The things he said to them were unprintable.

In his column a few days later, he wished his daughter luck.

Lawless sued for divorce and alimony in Massachusetts, alleging cruel and abusive treatment. It was also charged that the marriage was never consummated. He blamed this on Walter Winchell. Eventually an annulment was obtained.

Then William Cahn began courting Toni Eden, and many lives were to be affected.

Cahn, a pleasant, ambitious young man, had just finished a four-year enlistment in the Army. Now he was casting his first Broadway play, "Devil's Galore."

His director, Bob Perry, suggested that he see Toni Eden in "Dark of the Moon" which Perry had also directed.

Cahn signed Toni Eden for the ingenue lead.

The show lasted only three weeks. But not until Winchell made a unique public appearance with his wife. The couple came to see the show.

Afterwards, Cahn escorted them backstage to Toni's dressing room. The foursome chatted about the theatre in general. Mrs. Winchell was the typical proud parent.

Winchell gave the show encouraging notices and after it closed he told producer Cahn that he was "a brave man to gamble on my daughter's talent as an actress."

By this time, unknown to Winchell, Toni Eden and Bill Cahn were a steady twosome. Because of her past experiences, Tony didn't invite her new flame to her home or mention him to her father.

The two were walking along Fifth Avenue one afternoon when they ran into Winchell. The columnist was quite charming. He kissed his daughter, shook hands with Cahn, and invited the two of them to accompany him to the entrance of the Stork Club where they left him.

That night, or rather in the following early morning, Winchell sped to his Westchester estate, stamped into his daughter's room and wakened her. He quizzed her for hours until she finally admitted that she was fond of Bill Cahn.

Winchell went into a rage from which he has seemingly never recovered.

He sent out word to his press agents that he wanted "dirt" of any nature about Cahn.

He got the dirt. Cahn had pleaded guilty to a misdemeanor in 1935, and on another occasion had spent six days in a Florida jail. The severe charge? Vagrancy.

That was enough for Winchell. He secured Cahn's police identification card (the so-called Rogues' Gallery photograph) from a corrupt police official and waved it at Toni.

"You give this guy up. Do you understand?" he shouted at her.

Before he could finish his gloating act, Toni interrupted: "I knew all about that police business. Bill mentioned it to me when we first started going together."

Winchell showed obvious surprise.

"Well," he grunted finally, "you'll stop seeing him as of this minute or I'll fix him good."

He tried to convince her that Cahn was interested in her only to "get in good" with Winchell. It is typical of Winchell's maladjustment that he couldn't believe that anyone would be interested in his daughter for her own sake.

(On another occasion Winchell told her he knew for sure that Cahn "represented the mobs" and was going with her to "get something" on him.)

Toni Eden was neither moved by this nor by the hysterical scenes which followed. She knew her father: knew that because he was her father, Broadway felt sorry for her.

In the Stork Club, he would wave Cahn's Rogues' Gallery photo and tell anyone who would listen what he was going to do to Cahn.

Winchell did everything to wreck Cahn's life. He had Cahn followed day and night. Cahn produced three additional Broadway shows, "I Like It Here," "Darling, Darling, Darling," and "Toplitsky of Notre Dame," and Winchell panned them all unmercifully.

If Cahn stayed at a hotel, Winchell would attack the hotel as a "hangout for ex-convicts."

When Cahn went into business, Winchell did what he could to smear any innocent people connected with it.

However, though Winchell talked about "that convict producer," he never mentioned Cahn by name in his column or on the air.

He was always worried that despite his efforts, Toni would marry Cahn. And that he would have built himself into "the father-in-law of an ex-con."

Toni and Bill had become Winchell's "ace in the hole." Whenever he found a new romantic interest of his own, he would journey to his rarely visited mansion at Scarsdale and create a big scene with June.

He usually ended with his, "I'm never coming back here again."

Then he was off to his current romantic interest. Sometimes the location was Florida, sometimes Hollywood. Or he would just check into the Waldorf for a week until his ardor cooled.

Around Broadway (or Hollywood, or Miami Beach or Las Vegas) the gag among hip people was, "If you want to know who Walter's new girl is you look for the girl who is in his party but with a press agent as official escort."

There was a joke too about the press agent who was caught "cheating" by his wife but who successfully explained the misadventure by saying, "But dear, you know I'm fronting for Walter."

One morning at 3 a.m., Toni called Bill and asked him to meet her.

When they met she was shaking. She explained that her father had threatened to kill her, that he'd gone beserk and pulled his gun. She'd run from the apartment.

Cahn called Toni's Aunt Mary. Cahn and the Aunt tried to convince Toni that it would be all right to go home. Toni was adamant, and then confided to Bill other reasons, all logical, for not wanting to be left alone with her father.

She checked into the Belmont-Plaza under her mother's maiden name, McGee.

Cahn and Toni, despite everything that had gone before, were unprepared for what was to come.

28

"Our Daughter Is Missing"

Shortly before Thanksgiving Day, 1947, Walter Winchell visited his home to pick up a scrapbook of his old columns.

"Have you broken Toni and that bum up yet?" he asked his wife.

"Why don't you let them alone," June said. "It may wear off if you let them alone."

"It's got to be ended now. Once and for all."

"No," June said, "it doesn't have to be ended. If we leave them alone—"

"Are you insane? Do you want her to marry that heel?"

"How do you know he's a heel? Have you ever talked with him?"

The columnist gave an ultimatum to his wife. It was her job to break up the romance. No expense was too great. But under no condition was his name to be dragged in. Winchell desired to avoid unfavorable publicity.

June's first reaction to the ultimatum appeared to be dismay. She had resigned herself to the probable marriage. She sent Cahn gifts without Winchell's knowledge. The year before she'd given him an expensive Christmas present.

But now her attitude changed.

According to sworn testimony on file with the New York State Supreme Court, a series of events then took place which must rank as unique in the annals of parental love.

June Winchell went to the Gotham Hotel in Manhattan where Toni was living and told the assistant manager, "I'm Mrs. Walter Winchell. I'm going to remove my daughter from this hotel and I want your cooperation."

It was too much for the assistant. He called the manager who told her, "Madam, if she wants to go with you voluntarily—"

"Just keep your nose out of my affairs, or my husband will make plenty of trouble for you."

A few minutes later, Cahn received a phone call from Toni. She cried into the phone, "Bill, please come over here right away. They're trying to take me away! Please come right away!"

Before Cahn could reply, another voice came over the wire. "Bill Cahn, this is Mrs. Winchell. Don't you dare come near here or I'll have you arrested!"

In the background, Cahn could hear Toni's voice saying again, "Please come, Bill! Please come!"

The receiver was slammed down at the other end.

Cahn lived a block away from the Gotham. He sprinted to the hotel. An ambulance was parked at the hotel entrance.

At Toni's floor, he found Mrs. Winchell and two of the hotel managers in front of Toni's door. A couple of bellhops were also loitering in the corridor.

Mrs. Winchell hurried over to Cahn as he stepped from the elevator. "Don't you dare go in there, Bill Cahn. We don't want you near her. Don't you dare go near that door."

June Winchell didn't look "quite right" to Cahn and he tried talking to her very gently. "Mrs. Winchell, I don't know what this is all about. Can't we talk it over quietly and maybe I can be of some help?"

June Winchell seemed unable to control her hysteria. "No," she said. "We are taking her away. We are putting her away."

At that moment Toni walked from the room, followed

by a male nurse. "Please come inside, Bill," Toni said. The male nurse followed them into the room.

"What's happening, Toni?" Cahn asked.

"My mother called and asked if I would be here at two o'clock because she had something important to talk to me about. When she came in she looked very pale and upset to me and I said, 'Mummy, what's the matter with you?' and she answered, 'Walda, you are sick, you are sick, you are crazy' and she went over and closed the windows.

"I said, 'What's the matter with you, mother? You look so pale. You look all upset.' Then she opened the door and let this nurse in and said, 'You are crazy. You are crazy, and don't do anything. I am taking you away.'"

Cahn advised Toni to call her lawyer, John Sperry. She did and Sperry said he would be over immediately.

While they waited, Winchell's lawyer Ernest Cuneo could be seen nervously pacing the corridor through the door which Toni had flung open.

Cuneo approached Cahn. He said the Winchells wanted to place Toni in an institution.

"There's nothing wrong with her," Cahn said.

"She's a little nervous," Cuneo said.

"She's crazy!" June Winchell kept repeating.

When Sperry arrived he told Toni that as a married woman (her annulment hadn't come through yet) she was free to do what she wished and that marriage had emancipated her from her parents.

While Sperry argued with Cuneo, Bill Cahn and Toni quietly eluded the male nurse and escaped from the apartment.

They walked along Park Avenue to the Waldorf-Astoria. In the Peacock Alley of the Waldorf, the couple ordered drinks while Cahn tried to assure Toni that it would "work out all right."

At one point Toni told Cahn, "He drove Mother to do this. He's threatened me with it many times. I've been afraid of my father all my life."

It was decided that Toni would stay with some married friends out of the city.

A few days later, Gabriel Heatter went on the air saying, "Tonight, the sympathies of the nation are with Mr. and Mrs. Walter Winchell. Their daughter Walda has disappeared."

On the air that Sunday, Winchell announced, "This is one helluva Thanksgiving. Our daughter Walda is seriously ill and missing."

Cahn kept away from his own apartment for a few days. But after Winchell's announcement he decided to visit Toni's lawyer, John Sperry at the Belmont Plaza Hotel.

He almost walked into a trap. As he was about to step into an elevator in the hotel lobby, a bell-hop motioned to him.

"Mr. Cahn, you've been a right guy. I want to warn you. If you're going to see Mr. Sperry, he's surrounded by detectives, lawyers and Mrs. Winchell. I think they're tapping his phone wire too. At least that's what I hear."

Cahn thanked him, tipped him, and then went to a telephone booth in a nearby drug store.

Sperry finally persuaded him to meet with Cuneo.

Cahn waited in a doorway at Lexington Avenue and 86th Street watching the car approach. He wanted to make certain that there was no one present other than the two attorneys.

Cuneo convinced Sperry and Cahn that if Toni came in under the writ she would have full protection inasmuch as the writ was answerable to the widely-known and respected Judge Ferdinand Pecora.

Cahn called Toni and expressed his belief that Pecora could be trusted and was beyond Winchell's reach.

At one a.m. that morning, Sperry and Cahn met Toni, and the three went to Judge Pecora's apartment.

To their surprise, in addition to Mrs. Winchell and Judge Pecora, they were met by two psychiatrists. The psychiatrists were bowing and scraping before Mrs. Winchell. Cahn told Sperry he was afraid they would sign anything they were asked to sign.

However Toni appeared calm. She told a straightforward story. Her agitation was only over the knowledge that her parents were stopping at nothing to break up her romance. The Winchell plan seemed to be to commit her to a sanitarium and so write finis to her relationship with Cahn.

At one point Judge Pecora had a private heart-to-heart session with Toni which lasted almost two hours, while the others waited in the outer room.

When they joined the others Toni whispered to Cahn, "Bill, he's going to dismiss the case. He knows there's nothing wrong with me. Everything is okey."

It was five a.m.

Suddenly Mrs. Winchell asked to see the Judge alone.

When they came out of their huddle Judge Pecora said, "Toni, will you do something for me."

"Yes, Judge Pecora. What is it?"

"Will you go of your own volition to the Regent Nursing Home? You're tired. It's almost six o'clock. You need a good rest. No one will bother you. We will allow a few days for your Mr. Cahn to get a psychiatrist of his own. Then we will have a hearing."

Toni stared unbelievingly at the famous jurist. (A few years later he was to fail badly in his attempt to become the Mayor of New York. He was to fail despite Walter Winchell's many and enthusiastic plugs for his candidacy.)

Toni turned to her Mother. "Mother, will you tell me what is inside of you to do this to me? What has my father done to you? Why are you doing this to me?" There were tears in her eyes.

Mrs. Winchell began to weep. She buried her face in her hands, sobbing uncontrollably.

Toni sighed. "I'll go to the rest home," she said. "But I'll only go if the Judge will promise that my father won't come near me."

Attorney Cuneo told her that Winchell was currently in Hollywood.

"All right," Toni said. "I'll submit to a mental examination."

Toni voluntarily entered Regent Hospital.

The following day was a Sunday and Cahn and Toni talked on the phone a few times.

Winchell's attorney protested the various psychiatrists that Sperry suggested. Everything drifted until Tuesday.

Then it happened.

Cahn learned that Toni had been removed from the Regent Hospital, bound and gagged.

He worked day and night to learn where she'd been taken. Judge Pecora brushed aside all inquiries with the flat statement that "Custody has been given to the parents." He never called the second hearing that he had promised to call, and would answer no questions about Toni's whereabouts.

Upon hearing that Toni was missing, William Lawless called Bill Cahn. Lawless was still married to Toni at the time. He asked Cahn if there was anything he could do. Cahn explained what had happened and Lawless came to New York from Boston.

A fighting attorney, Edward H. Levine, took the case.

He served June Winchell with a writ ordering her to produce Toni.

She consulted with Cuneo and the two immediately called Walter who was in Hollywood.

They asked Winchell to return to New York. He refused. June called him a sneak and a coward. She talked about his personal affairs, threatened to divorce him, became hysterical.

Winchell too became hysterical.

He promised that after "this" was all over, he would return to the East and stay put.

Nothing that Cuneo or June Winchell would say had any effect on Winchell.

The columnist, who was later to become the great advocate of opening whorehouse and vice trials to the public now warned Cuneo that their business relationship would be ended if a word of the case got into the newspapers.

"For God's sake, keep this whole thing quiet," Winchell pleaded, from three thousand miles away.

The scene which took place in the confines of the New York State Supreme Court was a strange one. There were no photographers present. No newspaper reporters.

Winchell didn't "item" the news in his column.

Through Toni's husband, William Lawless, William Cahn had brought a habeus corpus suit.

The legal document was titled:

Walda Winchell Lawless
Vs.
June Winchell

Toni had gone voluntarily to the Regent Nursing Home at 115 East 61 Street in Manhattan.

On December 2nd, two henchmen employed by the Winchell family went to the nursing home, seized Toni, beat her when she resisted, bound her and carried her to a waiting private ambulance. Like the weak plot of a grade "B" movie, she was thus "spirited away."

At the habeus corpus hearing, Cahn and Lawless tried to force June Winchell to produce her daughter. They charged that Toni was taken from the hospital in a straight-jacket. When she was carried out, her face was bloody.

The doorman of the rest home, John T. Quintelle, testified that it was not a straight-jacket in the technical sense of the word, but that her legs were strapped to a stretcher and her arms were strapped across her chest.

When Toni had been carried to the ambulance, one of her kidnappers handed the doorman a dollar bill. It was wet with blood.

Quintelle also reported that a nurse had told him: "Anybody ask you any questions about this ambulance yesterday, you don't know nothing."

Cahn told the judge: "I know that child has been in jeopardy. Her very life has been in jeopardy . . ." He later said, "When all this happened I was feeling very frightened in view of the powers of the Winchell name and family."

June didn't deny that because of Toni's affair with Cahn, Winchell wouldn't have his own daughter in his house.

In response, the Winchell lawyers claimed they had "followed the advice of eminent and distinguished doctors whose findings have been further confirmed by an independent physician of unquestioned professional ability and integrity . . . that the infant Walda Winchell is in need of hospitalization and care . . ."

Cuneo charged that Cahn was bringing the action "as a nuisance and for purposes of embarrassment to . . . Winchell for sinister motives . . ."

He insisted that Toni was a "voluntary" patient "pursuant to section 71 of the Mental Hygiene Law of New York State . . ." and that "she is now in one of the finest institutions in the State."

Cuneo further charged that under "section 204 of the Insanity Law, the court has no jurisdiction here . . ."

Said another Winchell lawyer, "The purpose of this writ is for Walter (sic) Cahn to get hold of her again."

If an innocent girl's welfare were not at stake, some of the exchanges between the lawyers would have seemed comical.

Cuneo (to Cahn's lawyer, Edward H. Levine): "You are no medical authority."

Levine: "Neither are you."

Cuneo: "We produced more authorities than you can."

It was pointed out by Cahn's attorney that he had brought the action on Friday afternoon so no newspapers would get hold of the story.

Levine then asked: "Will your Honor direct them to

now disclose where she is so we can find out for ourselves whether she is voluntarily—"

"Never!" shouted June Winchell.

Who would shortly thereafter require psychiatric care herself.

The judge eventually learned that Toni was a patient at the Craig Institute at Beacon, New York.

He claimed to have spoken to her on the phone and reported that she now agreed to stay at the institution.

The habeus corpus action was dismissed.

Something deeper than reason seemed to make Winchell rebel against the thought of any man touching his daughter.

Nevertheless, when Toni was released from the institution, she resumed her friendship with Cahn.

"Look, kid," Cahn said, "when the buzzard dies, you'll inherit a couple of million. But the way things are going he'll cut you out of his will. If I stop seeing you maybe he'll let you alone. And he'll let me make a living."

Toni reminded him of the story about the pig who asked a cow, "Why does everybody love you and call me just a dirty pig when I give so much more than you?" and the cow answered, "Maybe because I give while I'm alive."

After nearly five years of keeping company, the pair finally did call it quits.

Then, in 1953, Cahn made what proved to be a tactical error. He married another woman.

Once the threat that Cahn would maybe be his son-in-law was cancelled out, Winchell was quick to take his revenge.

Cahn's name was mentioned in the Jelke trial.

(Unknown to Winchell, Cahn had been granted immunity during the time he testified to the Grand Jury.)

Winchell went to the office of the New York District Attorney to demand that Cahn be locked up.

"He traffics in women," Winchell said. "He's worse than Jelke."

"So what was your daughter doing with him for five years," an assistant district attorney asked.

Winchell stormed out of the D.A.'s office and added another to the hundreds of feuds he was carrying on.

He ran item after item in his column attempting to smear District Attorney Hogan and Assistant D.A. Scotti.

(Example from the column of March 4th: ". . . legalities are feverishly working on a 'hot tip' that one of Frank Hogan's staff was a pay-girl 'John'!"

(The column of that day also had four synthetic items about Scotti, all nasty.)

In February, a dull Winchell column on the Jelke case contained this item:

One of the customer-producers—an exconvict (W. C.) named by Miss Pat Ward gets a monthly disability check from Uncle Sam for being mentally unstable. Never in combat. Four raps on his criminal record. Did a stretch in the pen. The Jelke defense counsel has his record. Clipped B'way pals for a bundle producing flops.

(The item was fanciful, to say the least. But since Winchell didn't "name names" it would be difficult to prove he meant Cahn.)

However, he hoped that his Sunday television audience might tie one and one together. On Sunday he held up the Rogues' Gallery photo.

"This dirty four letter word," he snarled, bouncing up and down in his seat, "this four letter word calls himself Billy Cahn. But he isn't the fighter. His name is really Cohen."

Cahn was on his way to Florida with his bride when the stunt took place.

When he returned to New York he phoned Toni.

Her first words were: "Be careful, Bill, I think my phone is tapped."

"I'm going to sue him, Toni, and I'm afraid you'll be dragged into it—"

"Do what you have to do, Bill. I begged him not to do it."

(By now, Toni Eden was talking to her father again. Unable to get a show business job because of the stigma attached to the Winchell name, she acts as a helper on the television show. Winchell pays her about $100 a week in addition to her allowance of about another hundred.)

Winchell repeated the Cahn item almost daily, with variations.

On February 13, for instance, he ran this:

. . . One of Jelke's legal staff told reporters in the corridor that a "customer and procurer" named on the stand by Pat Ward was a Bill Cahn. The papers spelled it with a K instead of a C. His right name is Cohen. He has a criminal record. Rogues' Gallery photos, etc. Carried cards saying he with the Henry ('he's my pal') Rosenfeld firm which is strictly a front in case of another arrest for vagrancy, etc.

From then on, Winchell added dress and cosmetics manufacturer Henry Rosenfeld to his list of hates.

When he learned that Rosenfeld was friendly with Mayor Vincent Impellitteri, he also shot a stream of invective at the Mayor.

Since the items were a product of Winchell's or his press agents' imaginations, Winchell used initials rather than names.

On March 4, for instance, he wrote that a lawyer hoped to get his job back as a Magistrate "by laying off H. R., an involved intimate of a High City Initial."

With Winchell, it was a never ending chain of hatreds.

29

When Hatehood Was in Flower

Some years ago, in a Cotton Club review, Cab Callaway sang a new song titled "What Goes Up, Must Come Down."

Winchell's comedown was coming up.

The scandal in his private life had remained private. His income was the highest. His column was now reaching more than six hundred newspapers a week. Once, when he heard that his network (then called "The Blue Network") was in financial trouble, he went to the office of its president, Edward Noble, and offered to produce two million dollars of his own in cash by noon the next day, in return for a share of the company.

"I could have scraped up another million if I had to," he boasted.

Winchell was up. High.

The Winchell crash began on the night of October 16, 1951.

On that night, an internationally known singer named Josephine Baker, who was then playing to packed houses at the Roxy Theatre in New York, decided to visit the Stork Club with three friends.

Miss Baker and one of the friends were Negroes.

The four were seated in the Cub Room. Winchell sat nearby. The two white members of the party were served. Miss Baker was given the notorious Stork Club freeze treatment. Her order was taken but no food or drink was served to her.

After enough time had elapsed for everybody in the room to be very conscious of what was going on, Winchell told a companion: "I'm getting out of here. I don't want to get mixed up in this."

He left.

To Winchell's way of thinking, he had "cleared himself" by not being around for the full Jim Crowing of Josephine Baker.

It was not the first time the Stork Club's racial snobbery had been a source of embarrassment to the columnist.

For years people had called his attention to the strange treatment the Stork Club gave to Jewish patrons. One night in Lindy's restaurant, he overheard a real estate operator named William Lipman talking to some friends about what he called "the Winchell-Billingsley mutual brown-nosing society."

Winchell flung a catsup bottle at Lipman. It struck the realtor on the forehead.

Winchell ran out of the restaurant, knocking over a water pitcher, two chairs, and dropping his hat in his mad rush to get away. Lipman pursued him but was unable to catch the columnist.

Lipman required several stitches.

Winchell was waiting at the police station when Lipman arrived. The columnist threatened to file charges of "using foul and abusive language" against Lipman if Lipman filed an assault charge against him.

No charges were filed.

There were other similar incidents. But none was costly to Winchell, who continued to pose before his public as a self-styled defender of minority groups.

The interesting part about the Josephine Baker incident is that it showed Winchell had become a hypocrite in his own public "racial attitudes." So much so that now, when he began to slip badly on the banana peel of race prejudice, he thought he was floating through the air like a knight on a magic carpet.

Shortly after the Baker incident, a Negro prize-fighter named Sugar Ray Robinson tried to take Winchell's side, but admitted to a reporter: "Winchell advised me never to come to the Stork Club. He told me I'd be embarrassed and probably turned away."

Two newspapers had carried the story of the Baker snub. An after-midnight commentator on a local New York station had permitted Miss Baker to tell her side of the story.

In a behind-the-scenes agreement made by his attorney, Winchell agreed to condemn the Stork Club discrimination in return for a letter from the National Association for the Advancement of Colored People praising his "record" of opposition to bigotry.

As could have been expected, Winchell double-crossed the NAACP. He read their letter and then condemned those who were "trying to involve me in an incident in which I had no part."

NAACP Director Walter White promptly attacked Winchell for the sneak tactic.

The Negro press front-paged the story.

For a short time it seemed as though Winchell would score another Walter Winchell victory; that the incident would blow over and be forgotten.

Two weeks after the Baker incident, a couple of editors were putting the last-minute touches to the second issue of their new publication.

It was a monthly tabloid. It promised to publish stories and articles that most newspapers, fearing advertising cancellations or pressure group reprisals, would shy away from.

Winchell was a whole pressure group in himself. For years, the press had been curiously reluctant to criticize this most powerful of columnists. Even in L'affair Stork, there was hardly any criticism of Winchell outside of the Negro press.

The monthly tabloid was called *Exposé*. It began with $1,400 capital. The lead story in the first issue had exposed Allen Zoll, a professional hate-peddler who was stirring up a mixture of smears against the nation's public schools.

The second issue lead story was to be headlined "The Mysterious Mr. Matthews." It was to chronicle an amazing network of Negro-baiters and Jew-baiters who depended for their ideas upon as unsavory a character as had ever worked (behind the scenes) for William Randolph Hearst.

J. B. Matthews would become a national scandal when appointed an executive on the McCarthy committee. His smear against the Protestant ministry would cause President Eisenhower to condemn him, and force his resignation.

But that was not to happen for nearly two years, and now J. B. Matthews was virtually unknown except among the crackpot fringe who idolized him.

The first issue of *Exposé*, distributed by the newsdealers' own association, was being poorly displayed on newsstands. Its sales were disappointing.

The J. B. Matthews issue was scheduled to go to press in two days.

It was a Tuesday night at 9:30 when the editors of *Exposé* walked out of the Chanin Building on Forty-Second Street where they had been attending a broadcast.

Managing Editor Joseph Whalen bought a copy of the next day's *Daily Mirror*, which goes on midtown newsstands at eight o'clock on the previous evening.

Winchell had already obviously wrecked the career of Josephine Baker in the United States. There would be no future night club or theater bookings for Miss Baker in her native land.

He had, for instance, implied that she was a "fascist" by quoting a statement she is reported to have made about Mussolini in 1935.

In the next column he took out his red typewriter ribbon. Now she wasn't a "fascist"—she was that other kind of "ist"—a "fellow-travelist."

He didn't say "communist" for that is libelous per se. But the implications were plain. He labeled her protest "riot incitement."

As the two *Exposé* editors scanned the Winchell column, the editor turned to his managing editor.

"Joe, do you remember when Winchell was against making bad jokes based on racial stereotypes?"

(On his broadcast of January 12, 1947, Winchell had said: "If you hear of any comics—I call them vomics—who use jokes offensive to any race or people, please let me know. I am going to ridicule them right off the stage . . .)

"I remember," Joe Whalen said.

"Look at this one."

The two men read and re-read in the Winchell column one of the foulest anti-Negro jokes any newspaper had ever published. It was complete with blackface dialect.

"This is a new low," the editor said. "Someone ought to do something about this."

"Like what?"

"Someone ought to tell the Winchell story. The true story. He's fooled so many millions of people for so long . . . and now this new low . . ."

Within an hour the two men had decided to postpone the J. B. Matthews series for one month.

The editor went to his office and worked through that night without sleep. By morning, a rough draft of the Winchell story had been written.

In the morning, Managing Editor Joe Whalen went to work checking facts.

By two in the afternoon, a second draft had been written. By seven that night, a final draft had been written and corrected and mailed to the printer, marked "rush."

Later, the rumor was to spread that the editor had done a "hatchet-job" on Winchell because the columnist had angered him personally. But actually Winchell had mentioned the editor twenty or thirty times and always favorably.

Later, too, the rumor would spread that the editor had been a legman on Winchell's payroll and was bitter over being fired, etc. But the editor never worked for Winchell.

The beginnings of the first legitimate exposé of Winchell could honestly be traced to a gutter-type joke about Josephine Baker and Negroes generally.

Perhaps no one is better able to say that with authority than the author of this book, who was that editor.

Exposé went to press on Thursday. Its headline was "The Truth About Winchell." It was delivered to the distributor on Friday. But on the following Monday, copies were not to be found on any newsstand.

The publisher of *Exposé* was told by a Newsdealers' Association employee: "The boss said not to deliver the papers to the newsstands."

The "boss" was Association President William Richter, a politically ambitious attorney.

He had sent copies to Winchell's office, together with a telegram in which he said, "I want to assure you that I shall not distribute this paper."

He gave orders not to return the undelivered papers to the publisher.

Word about the obvious attempt to gain Winchell's favor by suppressing the paper reached *Time* magazine, which began an investigation. This caused Richter to release the papers to the publisher after first having mutilated three thousand of them with mimeograph ink.

With few subscribers and no newsstand distribution, the future of *Exposé* seemed bleak.

The editors decided to act as their own distributors. With bundles of papers under each arm, they trudged down Broadway, leaving a quantity at each newsstand.

At Kid Herman's on Times Square, they left one hundred copies. Exhausted, and depressed, they returned to their office on Fifty-Fifth Street.

They arrived just in time to answer a telephone call.

"Hello. You got any more of those papers?" the voice at the other end asked.

"Who is this?"

"This is Kid Herman's newsstand. We could use some of those papers."

"But we left a hundred with you about thirty minutes ago."

"We're almost sold out. You better bring some more."

By noon the next day, Kid Herman's sold an additional three hundred copies. Other newsstands began calling in that morning. A new printing of *Exposé* was ordered. Then another. And another.

Kid Herman's news stand alone sold 1,450 copies in two weeks. This is many times more than they'd ever sold of any national magazine.

Before demand for the Winchell issue subsided, more than 85,000 would be printed and distributed.

Later, when the Newsdealers Association of Greater New York held its annual election, William Richter, who had tried to suppress *Exposé*, was not reelected president.

The editors of *Exposé* had a copy of the Winchell issue delivered to Walter Winchell by messenger.

The columnist was in Florida. He'd embarked for Jim Crow Miami Beach three weeks ahead of schedule, in order to avoid the heat of the Baker controversy.

Winchell received his copy at two o'clock on Tuesday. At four o'clock he was on a plane to New York.

He didn't delay long enough to pack any baggage. Under his arm when he ran for the plane at Miami Airport was a single crumpled copy of *Exposé*.

Winchell refrained from mentioning *Exposé* by name. But in New York the word went out that he would be "gratefully appreciative" for any "dirt" about the editor of that paper.

He attacked the editor at length on his Sunday broadcast. Like much of what Winchell broadcasts as personal reprisal, the attack made no sense to many of his listeners. To anyone who hadn't seen a copy of *Exposé*, it sounded as if Winchell were angry at three guys named Oogoo at the North Pole for not subscribing to the *Reader's Digest*. Or something like that.

A few weeks later, reporters from three newspapers had come to *Exposé* for help in preparing a series of articles.

A reporter from the *New York Post* spent most of two days at the *Exposé* office, getting names, tips, telephone numbers, and being shown documentary evidence to support the *Exposé* story.

"We're going to do a series on Winchell and I thought I would come here first," he said.

Other newspapers and magazines also did articles critical of Winchell. Of these, the *Jewish Daily Forward* and the *Afro-American* gave credit to *Exposé* for much of their source material.

The *Post* series was in its fourth week when it was announced that Walter Winchell was suffering from a "heart attack" and had been ordered to cease his column and broadcast immediately.

The next issue of *Exposé* revealed that the "heart attack" was in truth a psychological crackup. The criticism had made Winchell a nervous wreck.

It was his third nervous breakdown in thirty years.

30

Free for All

Two weeks before the fatal Josephine Baker incident, Winchell had signed a lifetime contract with the American Broadcasting Company. Its terms were that he was to receive more than a half million dollars a year, plus a chunk of stock from his then-current sponsor plus a chunk of stock in the network—all in return for his services on radio and television.

Two years later, the man who signed that contract, ABC President Robert Kintner, listened to friends tell him that he had made a mistake.

Within those two years, much had happened. Not much of what had happened was good for Winchell.

After many months of temporary retirement following his breakdown, Winchell returned to the air. But just before a Sunday broadcast he told his announcer, "I just can't make it. I'm sick to my stomach. I just can't make it."

The announcer went on in his stead.

This anticlimactical breakdown was described by his secretary as "exhaustion following a serious attack of virus."

There were some who said Winchell was finished. Washed up. There was a little sympathy around Broadway for the columnist. And the old enemies he'd made breathed a sigh of relief.

It is a peculiar fact that the majority of the people who feuded with Winchell were people who had once praised him, worked with him, defended him against his critics.

He could write with honest irony: "Boy, get me some Scotch-tape. I want to lengthen my list of ingrates."

Unfortunately, many of these people who had been tied to him were themselves vulnerable.

In many instances, the battles were examples of sending a boy to do a man's errand.

For Winchell returned again. And now he decided to ignore the advice given him before his breakdown that to attack back would dignify his critics.

(When some of the early exposures of him were being published, he ignored them, ending his Friday column with the remark: "Nothing exciting happening. Veddy soddy.")

But not mentioning the critics apparently had not damaged them. Now he went at them with a vengeance.

Few of the new enemies could honestly be accused of having looked for the fight.

The *New York Post* in an editorial explained that its series was "not basically a portrait of Winchell as a gossip columnist. We do not deplore his journalistic invention. Indeed, let us say at the outset that on several occasions . . . we have heard that Winchell was playing with the idea of joining the *Post;* we were happy to hear the news."

The *Post* couldn't criticize Winchell's "journalistic invention." It had three gossip columnists of its own.

Why then the series?

To gain new circulation, the *Post,* under editor James Wechsler, had frequently used what Wechsler himself described as "shock treatment." Sensationalism, sex and exaggeration had lured some morning tabloid readers to the afternoon *Post's* corral.

(One of the first questions the *Post* reporter asked on visiting *Exposé* was: "Your issue is a sellout, isn't it?"

Frequently in its series, the *Post* was as inaccurate as

Winchell. At other times, it was as knowingly hypocritical.

For example, the *Post* published a photograph of Winchell with newsman Johannes Steel and described Steel as "one of the Commies' pet writers on international affairs. He had Winchell's ear."

Guilt by association.

But the *Post* didn't point out that when the photograph was taken Steel was on the staff of—the *New York Post*.

Or that he had been foreign editor of the *Post* and years later contributed a regular column for the *Post*.

The *Post* pretended to be indignant because Winchell hadn't spoken in defense of Josephine Baker.

But the *Post* itself had frequently suppressed news stories when they concerned Palisades Park pool Jim-Crowing some war veterans. Suppressed all mention of the story—because the amusement park was an advertiser in the *New York Post*.

The *Post* tried to smear Winchell with a red brush by mentioning that he had been a sucker for the Communist-written book "Sabotage." It didn't mention that the entire book had been serialized in full, years before—in the *New York Post*.

The *Post* got its circulation increase. Some 30,000 new readers. Eighteen months later, the *Post* could boast an average daily circulation of 420,247.

But it could also look back on some unhappy results.

Wechsler and the *Post* (Winchell began calling it the "Compost") had been slandered by Winchell from coast to coast on radio and television and libeled in the column.

Wechsler, who years before had been a Communist, was described in the Winchell column as an ex-Communist . . . but always with quotes around "ex-Communist." Invariably, Winchell tied every newly identified Communist to Wechsler's tail. The average Winchell reader or listener waded through paragraphs about Soviet agents, Alger Hiss, the Rosenberg spies. And somehow, the name Wechsler kept bobbing up again and again.

In mid-December of 1952, the *Post* and editor Wechsler filed suits against Winchell and his employers, seeking to recover $1,525,000 in damages.

The *Post* and Wechsler felt they had been damaged at least that much.

In its complaint, the *Post* charged: "Defendant Winchell has long been notorious as a person who uses his journalistic position for the purpose of making reckless, untrue and libelous statements and as a personal weapon for the purpose of injuring and intimidating persons against whom he has personal enmity.

"With these tactics, defendant Winchell has engaged in a form of journalistic gangsterism. Defendant Winchell has used these tactics and stock in trade as a means of building up circulation and readership. Defendant Hearst, with knowledge of such fact, permitted and aided defendant Winchell to use such tactics . . ."

Winchell waited ten days. Then he sued back. He started a suit for $2,000,000 against the *Post* and Wechsler. Among the things he said the nasty *Post* had done to damage him: they had called him a liar.

At the pre-trial examination of the Wechsler-*Post* suits against him, Winchell described his column as gossip.

"It has always been gossip," he said.

"Is it still gossip?" the *Post* attorney asked.

"I would call it that. Yes."

"Do you credit yourself with having introduced the gossip column to American journalism?"

Winchell's answer was a simple "No."

Later in the examination another column was introduced as evidence. It had been written by Wechsler in 1944 in defense of Winchell for the Guild Reporter of the Newspaper Guild.

Winchell appeared genuinely touched.

"I never knew about that," he said. "I never saw it before."

The columnist also revealed that he had never met Wechsler; wouldn't know him if he stumbled over him in the Stork Club.

Winchell's second target had also not been looking for trouble. He was an after-midnight radio commentator named Barry Gray.

He had permitted Josephine Baker to relate her Stork Club trouble on his microphone. He had also "turned over" his microphone to gossip columnist Ed Sullivan for a one-hour scathing attack on Winchell. Sullivan, an old enemy of Winchell's since the two were fellow employees on the *Graphic,* told at length and in detail how much he "despised" Winchell.

Once, Winchell had angered Sullivan in Reuben's restaurant, and the athletic Sullivan had grabbed Winchell by the necktie, dragged his chin through a cheesecake that sat on the table, and shouted, "You son of a bitch, if you say one more word I'll take you downstairs and stick your head in the toilet bowl."

Winchell didn't say one more word. When Sullivan released him, Winchell's face was white.

He brushed some of the cheesecake from his neck and shirt and left.

Sullivan was delighted at the chance to lambast Winchell on the radio after all these years. His own home town newspaper, the *Daily News* usually cut all reference to Winchell, not wanting to build up the second-rate *Daily Mirror* which carried Winchell.

When Sullivan was finished, Gray announced that he "was taking no sides" and that he was offering Winchell equal time to appear at the WMCA microphone to answer his critics.

The *Post* had become "The New York Poo" and "The Postitute" in Winchell's column. Gray now became "Borey Pink," "Barry Yellow," "a disk jerk."

Press agents around town informed all entertainers that

if they appeared on the Gray show, they would go on Winchell's blacklist.

Gray was appearing in a restaurant named "Chandler's." Winchell called it "Chiselers" and treated the restaurant and its owner with malice until it dropped Gray.

Gray went into another restaurant. Again Winchell attacked. Gray was finally dropped and forced to broadcast from a radio studio.

Yet in the very beginning, on returning to the air after a vacation, Gray had announced, ". . . any further attack will be met with attack stronger and more lasting than tonight . . . lies will be met with the truth . . . low blows are going to be met with clean punches . . . If these innuendoes about me continue in Walter Winchell's column, I'm going to devote every moment that I can to fighting them on the air . . ."

The innuendoes continued. Gray was unable to live up to his pledge of retaliation.

The first serious criticism of Gray had been made by the *Post*'s own radio columnist Paul Denis, in 1948. Now the *Post* took Gray in its arms and sheltered him. His column became an every-day-but-Friday feature.

Unfortunately for all concerned, even with the help of a ghost, Gray's talent was not on the side of columning.

Ed Sullivan, who knew when to get out of the rain, devoted himself to his column and television show. If he did anything to assist Gray, it didn't show publicly.

Time magazine wrote: "The motives that move columnist Walter Winchell's wormlike thrusts are mysterious to the average man—but not so mysterious to those who feel the pressure of his vermiform 'journalism.'"

Winchell turned his popgun on *Time*, its press editor, and even its publisher's wife.

He wrote:

The setback in the Italian elections is blamed on Ambassador Clare Luce, whose speeches were not authorized.

He was feuding with everybody. With the *New York Times* and its publisher Arthur Hays Sulzberger. With the Pulitzer Prize Committee for never having recognized him even with a dunce prize. With his old editor on both the *Graphic* and the *Mirror*, Emile Gauvreau. With *Time* magazine. The *New York Post*. Columnists Leonard Lyons, Earl Wilson, Ed Sullivan. With Barry Gray. With the *New Yorker* magazine. With Harry S. Truman. With Drew Pearson and Elmer Davis. With Arthur Schlesinger, Jr. With the book publishing industry. With Max Lowenthal. With Bennett Cerf. With a hundred others.

He was now writing with nothing but enmity in his heart. He was thrashing around in a mud puddle of petty hates.

He had turned against the New Deal. He hated the Democrats. He opposed Adlai Stevenson and had condoned filthy accusations, echoed every dirty charge and circulated every sewer falsehood against that Presidential candidate. He made a direct on-the-air appeal for votes for Eisenhower. The ABC network refused equal time to the Democrats.

He was the infallible opinionated oracle, setting the world on its course, giving the I'll-get-you-for-that treatment to any who got in his way or questioned his importance.

One of his pet petty hates was Bennett Cerf. Winchell felt that once a joke appeared in his column, it was his forever more and that furthermore he originated it. The truth, of course, is that the gag was given him by a press agent who swiped it from somebody else. Cerf also used gags. Winchell would snap at him with lines like:

If Bennett Cerf worked for a newspaper, his job would be "copy boy."

He battled the other gossip vendors.
Earl Wilson in his column carried this item:

Egomania Dept.: WW boasts of his April 6 "scoop" on the Milford-Haven split. Knickerbocker retorts he had the "scoop" Jan. 26. We had it Jan. 14. We're just a lowdown sneak."

Winchell became infuriated and showed it.

Meanwhile, among the vinegar drippings in the Winchell column would be the usual patter.

The political atonements like:

Sen. McCarthy is planning some surprising changes in his cast.

The wrong rumors like:

Are Nelson Rockefeller and Ike planning to hop to Africa?

He spelled Negroes with a small "n," used anti-Semitic touches ("Harry White alias Weiss") and veered more and more to the right.

"Colyumists Arthur Krock and David Lawrence (real Liberals) are among the most respected journalists," he wrote, pinning the tag "liberal" on Lawrence, one of the most reactionary writers in the country.

When a girlie magazine named *Confidential* published a story written by a Winchell press agent designed to smear Barry Gray, Winchell announced that the magazine was his favorite.

He also wrote:

One B'way and 50th Street stand (Cicero's) had an advance sale of 500 for Confidential mag, which debunks B'way's No. 1 Heel.

Cicero's reluctantly admitted to an *Exposé* reporter that they had no advance sale: received fewer than one hundred copies from the American News Company, sold less than half of these.

The reporter related the following exchange with the newsstand owner:

"Why did Winchell write that?"

"Do you believe everything you read? A publicity man asked me if I wanted publicity. Why not, I said."

(The other three 50th & B'way newsstands were

frankly anti-Winchell. The columnist had once falsely
written that they were each "making more than $1,500 a
week" causing the internal revenue agents to swarm
down on the struggling newsdealers who took weeks convincing the income tax men it wasn't so.)

In his column, Winchell wrote:

"Why don't you forget it," your friends tell you. "Life is too
short" . . . "That's the trouble," you reply, "it's too short. If it
were just a little longer, you might have time to get around to them
all."

31

Man Against the World

The listener heard a somewhat harsh voice pumping out gossip items in white-hot bursts, slowing down occasionally for emphasis. Winchell was at work again, agitating, stimulating the adrenal glands of his audience, turning every piece of ordinary information into a red-hot tip.

Winchell's news-slanting was often so distorted that it became humorous to the point of absurdity.

"Good evening, Mr. and Mrs. North and South America and all the ships at sea; let's go to press," he machine-gunned. And then he was off. Fracturing facts, wrecking marriages, ruining reputations, distorting history, perverting the press association news.

He was the same old Winchell. He had returned from the second breakdown in a year. And now he was paying off some debts.

Drew Pearson had replaced him on the 9 o'clock spot during Winchell's illness.

Now he helped to force Pearson out of ABC.

The two men had helped each other once, during the period when Winchell fancied himself a liberal.

Winchell had visited Drew Pearson's home in Washington: had dined with him often.

"Sometimes I wanted him to get to know a friend," Pearson told a reporter. "But he would talk all evening without letting the other fellow get a word in. He would talk about what he was going to do about his daughter and he would talk about himself."

(Producer Mike Todd once rode from Hollywood to New York on a train with Winchell and said that from the moment the train left until it pulled into New York, Winchell kept up a running conversation about himself, his importance and the important people he knew.

(Todd said that Winchell was able to talk even while eating without pausing.

("The only place I could escape his jawing was the men's room," Todd said. "Then after awhile he followed me there too. It was a hectic three days.")

(Todd's experience puts to shame the record of John Gunther who once tried to tell Winchell an anecdote but was unable to interrupt Winchell's monologue over a two and one-half hour period.)

Winchell helped McCarthy against Pearson by doing nothing. His was the guilt of the amused spectator rather than that of the dagger-holder.

Washington columnist Pearson was later able to set up a network of cooperative sponsors on independent stations. By mid-1953 he had more than 270 stations.

With Pearson gone, the Sunday night lineup of ABC news commentators consists of Walter Winchell, George Sokolsky and Paul Harvey, all of whom are reactionary enough to please the most avid Tory.

Wechsler of the *Post* wanted circulation. Gray didn't want to "get mixed up in anything" but wanted the publicity he thought would result from the use of his "free speech" microphone. Pearson pitied Winchell, didn't care to fight. The *New Yorker* refused to take Winchell seriously and often used his activities for comic relief.

Gossip columnist Leonard Lyons fought back. Like Gray and Wechsler, he underestimated Winchell, thought he could do battle on a level above the sewer.

For a time it seemed that Lyons was conducting himself with dignity.

He announced without explanation that he had resigned from Winchell's Damon Runyon Fund.

(This fund was a promotional scheme administrated by a race track tout, an ex-bootlegger, and Winchell, among others. It has collected and spent seven million dollars and its contribution toward relief or cure of cancer is nil to date.)

(It was typical of Winchell that he failed to do what a healthy commentator with an interest in cancer research might have done with a multi-million audience. He could have appealed for public support for a giant Congressional appropriation for cancer research. This might have stepped up a solution to cancer by years. But Winchell's ego couldn't conceive of doing anything for anybody unless there was plenty for Winchell in it; in this case, publicity and control of the funds.)

Lyons and Winchell had come to a parting of ways because the Lyons column appeared in the *New York Post*.

Winchell had helped Lyons get started as a columnist. He had given Lyons the title for his column. He had advised and assisted him for many years.

But now the duet had split.

Lyons was the only person approached who didn't cooperate with the author of this book.

On May 16th, he mailed a registered letter to the author in which he said in part: "I will be unable to talk to you about the biography of Mr. Winchell or participate in any way. Mr. Winchell and I enjoyed long years of friendship. I do not intend to violate any confidence he reposed in me. I would not do that to any man I know. I've written many things about him but none was a violation of confidence."

If Lyons had any illusions about resuming his servant-master relationship with Winchell, he was to discard them a few hours later.

After the letter had been mailed and postmarked, but before it arrived at its destination, another Winchell column appeared that loosed a long blast against Lyons. The diatribe concluded with:

He (Lyons) has since attempted to damage the Runyon Fund with half-truths, untruths and outright lies—because of his festering hate against this writer—who did everything possible to help him make good when he started a colyum . . . The insiders around town know all this . . . But the ingrate probably never went to bed without ending his prayers with: "And please let Winchell drop dead so I can get some new outlets" . . . When I was ill he went around town telling the lice I was "a very sick man" . . . He didn't mean I was sick with a virus . . . He has written letters about me (now in my possession) that would win a libel action and acquit me in a minute if I pushed him in front of a speeding truck.

What is left of his conscience keeps telling him: "You know very well you aren't chasing ambulances for a living only because Winchell was born! You swiped Walter's entire act but who hasn't? You are hateful for only one reason and it isn't because Walter couldn't stand you any longer on the Runyon Fund.

"You hate him because his colyum replaced yours in Washington. A horrible fate for a professional name-dropper."

Lyons tried to fight back.

At the end of his next column he carried this item:

"PERSONAL, to Police Commissioner Monaghan: I am about to write a series of replies to Walter Winchell's latest outburst about me—the one in which he concludes that he would be acquitted if he were to push me in front of a speeding truck. This, therefore, is public notice to you to pick up his permits and the pistol he carries, or else the City of New York shall be held accountable for any consequences. I write this not out of any concern for my own safety but only because, as Winchell himself has indicated, were he to pull a trigger in all probability he would hit either an innocent bystander or himself."

Like Barry Gray and like many others who had made courageous statements but weren't able to support them, Lyons never did get around to writing his "series of replies."

Wrote Winchell two days later: "Att'n, Police Comm.

Monaghan: The punk is so pink they called him Lenin."

Leonard Lyons had become just another steady target for the Winchell typewriter.

Winchell considered himself the foremost reporter of all times.

Two years ago he mentioned that he was looking forward to his next vacation, something he hadn't done when he was younger.

"Walter, you're getting old," a friend chided and added: "Listen, we know you're the King and there's nobody like you. But who do you think can ever take your place? I mean, who would you say is the Crown Prince?"

The friend proceeded to name some of the other gossip columnists. "Wilson (Earl Wilson)?" Winchell made an ugly face. "Kilgallen (Dorothy Kilgallen)?" He held his nose.

"There is no crown prince," he interrupted. "They all stink." Then he walked away, obviously annoyed.

The "friend" has not been mentioned in Winchell's column since.

But at that time Winchell could genuinely feel he was "the King."

For years, when he was attacked, he'd slap his attackers back and they'd crawl into the woodwork. Winchell's fire-power was devastating.

Now, they were saying he wasn't "the King" or even as nice a guy as he made himself out to be.

And they were able to get away with it.

Like an ex-champ who had become slightly punch drunk Winchell lashed out at the same hated people again and again.

Schopenhauer said "A word too much always defeats its purpose" and now Winchell revealed his weakness by the consistent pounding he had to give the same people. And more often than not, his worst blows were proving ineffectual.

32

The Undefeated

There are a few sure ways to get into Winchell's column and a few to stay out.

Here is the way one man stayed out.

Harry Evans, editorial director of Family Circle Magazine was seen by Winchell at the Stork Club. Evans and Ginger Rogers were eating a salad.

The next day Winchell wrote in his column that the two were being seen together. He spiced the item with romantic implications.

Evans cornered Winchell at the Stork Club bar a few nights later. "You know you've upset Ginger's mother and you've caused both Ginger and me a great deal of embarrassment," he said. "All we were doing was eating a salad. What would you write if you saw us eating a full course dinner together?"

Winchell mumbled something about having to go somewhere.

"Listen to me, Walter," Evans said. "If you ever mention me in your column again in any way whatsoever, I'm going to give you the thrashing of your life, and in front of all your Cub Room friends."

Winchell never mentioned Evans again.

He has a mortal fear of being beaten. Once he was attacked by assailants who to this day have remained unidentified. Winchell says they were Nazis.

He doesn't like to be kidded about it.

Winchell is the only thing that must be taken seriously at all times—according to Winchell.

Winchell has always been against press agents getting together. He would rather have them at each other's throat. It was to his advantage.

The fact that the Publicists' Guild managed to survive a few well-chosen snide remarks about itself in the Winchell column was aggravating to the columnist.

"What's the matter with you guys?" Winchell asked a press agent. "Don't you read my column?"

But the Publicists' Guild survived. And Winchell found a new reason to hate its President Ivan Black, a Harvard man.

The two weren't always enemies, though unlike most press agents, Black avoided Winchell. He never hung around the columnist or cow-towed to him.

For one thing, Black believed that gossip columns were important but that they were secondary to national magazines. For another thing, Black is a patron of the arts, of literature and of music. Winchell is blissfully ignorant on all of those counts.

In spite of these considerations, or maybe because of them, Winchell sought out Black when the publicity man was visiting Miami Beach in 1943. He introduced Black to people as "one of America's really great public relations men."

Black, in turn, was forced to sit on the beach and listen to the details of all of Winchell's feuds, especially the one involving Ed Sullivan.

One morning, a prominent banker was chatting with Black when Winchell came upon the scene. The banker had been describing something beautiful he'd seen early that morning. Cold air had hit the warm water of the Gulf Stream and created irregular wheels of mist all around the horizon. The rising sun painted the mist wheels with hugh patches of purple and gold.

Winchell listened as the banker repeated the description for his benefit.

"Sorry, I can't use it in my column" he said, and walked away.

"Nothing," quoted Black from Goethe, "is so terrible as ignorance with spurs on."

Thereafter Ivan Black avoided Walter Winchell as much as he could.

"He isn't my dish of ice cream," Black explained. "Deep down, the guy who has all this platform . . . all his audience . . . is hollow inside and he knows it. And knowing it is the basis of all his insecurity."

Black also made the classic remark: "Winchell's great frustration is that he hasn't been able to have children by himself."

As a fellow interested in political affairs, Black had an experience with Winchell he has never forgotten. On a Sunday night in 1946, he picked up a copy of the morning *Mirror* from a newsstand and then dropped into his favorite pharmacy for coffee.

The soda fountain radio was tuned in to Winchell.

Black listened with interest as Winchell attacked those who were calling for war with the Russians. The commentator assured his listeners that America would be at peace with Russia, and that those who said otherwise were little short of being traitorous.

Then Black opened his copy of the *Mirror* to page ten. There, to his surprise, he read in Winchell's column that war with Russia was inevitable, and that the United States would probably be at war with Russia within six weeks.

Amazed, he asked the man behind the soda fountain, "Say am I nuts or something? Did you listen to Winchell?"

"Sure."

"Did you hear him attack those who were calling for war with Russia?"

"Sure. I heard it. Why?"

"Read this," Black said.

The soda clerk read the column and scratched his head. "There must be something wrong somewhere," he said at last.

Black reported later: "It took me a while to figure out the answer. It was his ghost writers, of course. One had written the column and another had written the broadcast material, and neither knew what position the other had taken.

"It was incredible, but if a paperhanger could rule Germany, it isn't surprising that a second-rate hoofer could become America's oracle."

Black had worked for the *Boston Transcript*, the *Philadelphia Record* and the *Boston Post*. As an old newspaperman he was surprised one day to get a call from Winchell in which the columnist said: "I hear you're handling publicity for that Cahn fellow."

"Bill Cahn? I'm handling his new Broadway show."

"Drop it," Winchell commanded.

"I couldn't do that, Walter," Black replied. "I know about Cahn and your daughter but—"

He didn't have to continue. Winchell had hung up.

The next material Black sent Winchell for the column came back with the message "Stop sending me your stuff" scribbled across it in crayon.

So Black stopped sending Winchell his material. If he felt it necessary to get a client mentioned in the column, Black could rely on other press agents to do his planting for him.

Black thus became the first top-level press agent ever to be blacklisted by Winchell.

It didn't hurt much.

Two years later he was named "The Nation's Number One Star Maker" in the Sixth Annual Billboard magazine survey of press agents.

Winchell intensified the attack. He leveled a steady blast at Black. The usual smear innuendos became dirtier.

"The Senate probers (on Scummies) have subpena'd a press-agent we have been initialing for months," Winchell wrote. "He must appear today."

Or again: "The Publicists' Guild of B'way press-agents is in convulsions over many resignations because its President (Ivan Black) was subpena'd (for June 8th) before a Cong. Committee probing peculiars, etc."

Actually, Black's appearance before the Velde Committee has been delayed many times. At this writing he has not yet appeared.

As for the "many resignations": one was from Frank Law and the other from Ed Weiner.

These were the two who were at the short end of a 29 to 2 vote on whether Black should step aside as President of the Guild.

(Two others resigned at the next meeting. Their places were promptly taken by eighteen new members—many of them far more important in the public relations field than the four departees.)

That twenty-nine press agents were willing to stick together in defiance of Winchell was in itself a measure of the columnist's descent from the Gods.

Said Black after the overwhelming vote to support him: "Apparently Winchell is tired of playing Juliet to Sherman Billingsley's Romeo, and is now playing Dr. Goebbels to McCarthy's Hitler."

Winchell had two angles in the Jelke vice case.

One was that he hoped to embarrass William Cahn.

The other was that he hoped to embarrass Joey Adams. Adams, a comedian, had once made the mistake of marrying into the Winchell family. He had wed June Winchell's sister.

Worse, he had finally been divorced.

As punishment, Winchell never mentioned Adams in his column except in a derogatory way.

Even apart from the angles, it was natural for Winchell to become involved in the Jelke Case. Many of his personal friends were whores or pimps, or, as in the case of Sherman Billingsley, ex-bootleggers.

It has been said around Broadway that Winchell felt at home among whores because they, like Winchell, were selling themselves for so much a night.

In the same way it was natural that the Rockefeller brother Winchell became most friendly with was Winthrop, who had been sent to Polly Adler's house of prostitution at the age of sixteen to be taught that all things could be bought for money, and to be kept from the clutches of homosexuals who might have been attracted to the good looking but simple-minded rich man's son.

The Jelke case was a spectacular headline-maker. And as it received the front page splash positions in the tabloids, Winchell instinctively felt an urge to make himself part of the case.

He began by iteming initials in his column. He hated Leonard Lyons and so he mentioned that a columnist, initial "L," would be revealed as a patron of the pulchritude.

When he tired of making his enemies uncomfortable with the initial items, he decided to inject himself into the case personally.

His attempt to damage Cahn has been described earlier.

The opportunity to damage Joey Adams loomed in the absence of a girl named Grace Appel.

The Jelke defense was looking for Grace Appel to testify that she'd been at a wild party with call girl Pat Ward before Jelke knew Ward. The point was to prove that Pat was a fallen angel before Jelke became her pimp.

Winchell was interested because rumor had it that the so-called wild party had taken place in the Waldorf-Astoria suite of Joey Adams.

When the Jelke attorneys couldn't locate Grace Appel, the District Attorney's office offered to help.

Assistant D. A. Anthony Liebler who was prosecuting the Jelke case had an assistant named Bill Ryan.

One morning Ryan came looking for Liebler in his eighth floor office at 80 Leonard Street.

Liebler's secretary Arlene said the boss would be in in a few minutes.

Ryan waited impatiently until Liebler arrived.

"What's troubling you, Bill?" Liebler said when he saw the agitated look on his assistant's face.

"Boss man," said Ryan, "do you know what? Jelke's dumb bunny attorneys wanted to know if we are hiding Grace Appel!"

"What'd you tell them?" Liebler asked.

"Nothing I would want to repeat in front of Arlene," Ryan said.

The trio laughed and for a few hours, the Appel girl was forgotten.

At the reception desk on the eighth floor lobby, young Johnny had the assignment of clipping material from the newspapers. For years the Winchell column had been on the "don't bother to clip" list, and so neither Liebler nor Ryan knew that Winchell was telling Grace Appel to come in; to give herself up to him.

How much of herself she eventually gave to him was to become the subject of vaudeville comics' backstage gags for months.

Late that night a girl called Anthony Liebler's home. His wife answered the phone.

"This is Grace Appel," said a small voice. "I want to talk to your husband."

"He's in front of the house, I'll call him," said Mrs. Liebler. The girl at the other end began to cry.

"What's the matter my dear," said Mrs. Liebler.

"I'm crying because I'm so happy," said the girl. "I've spent almost twenty-four hours with Mr. Winchell. He's going to make me one of his daughters. I'm never going to leave him. I love him."

The phone at the other end clicked abruptly.

Mrs. Liebler sighed and went looking for her husband. Later she told him: "She was either a prankster, or that girl was drugged. It didn't sound normal at all."

When Winchell marched into court with Grace Appel the next morning, he made sure that the Hearst photographers were standing by.

"Hold it boys," he commanded. He combed his hair.

With a possessive confidence, he helped Grace straighten her skirt. "Okey, now you can shoot."

The flash bulbs made a halo of light as Winchell and Appel walked down the aisle.

He delivered Grace Appel to the defense attorneys.

They put her on the stand. She stumbled through what sounded to newsmen like rehearsed testimony. Carefully, the defense attorney, studying a slip of paper given to him by Winchell, drew from her the strange story that she had been in Joey Adams apartment in the Waldorf-Astoria Hotel some years before.

The boys had asked Pat Ward to join them in what is commonly known as a gang-bang.

Grace, a girlhood friend of Pat's, said she was shocked. She ran to the bathroom to perform minor tasks.

Pat Ward didn't remember. Nobody remembered. But if it happened it certainly would indicate that Pat was loose before Jelke allegedly corrupted her.

It was a very weak defense move and the defense attorneys were obviously uneasy about it. It was a long hard way to pull Joey Adams' name into the valley of whoredom.

Winchell sat back, grinning like a fat cat.

Then Liebler began his cross-questioning.

"Grace," he said, after a few preliminary questions, "did you ever call my wife and tell her that you were in love with Walter Winchell and wanted to stay with him as his child?"

Winchell shook his head no, and the girl, watching him, sobbed "No."

"Do you ever take dope?" Liebler asked.

"Only when I can't sleep," Grace Appel replied, apparently misunderstanding his question to mean sleeping pills.

Liebler dismissed the girl.

A few minutes later he walked over to Winchell and put his arm around Winchell's shoulder.

"Walter, I didn't intend any implication with that question. I just wanted to show the jury that the girl is a little, well, you know. She acted pretty crazy on the telephone."

"What about my wife?" Winchell blurted. "She's dying and you ask a question like that. What effect do you think it'll have on her?"

Later, Liebler recounted: "He didn't seem angry. He was thoughtful in a dull slow sort of way. I explained again that there was nothing personal. As I started to walk away he came after me."

"Will you write a letter and explain why you asked those questions?" Winchell asked.

Liebler said he would write the letter if it would help Winchell with his wife.

"She's almost dead," Winchell muttered. "This'll kill her."

Liebler reassured Winchell. He would make the letter very strong. There would be no chance for misunderstanding.

But Liebler never wrote the letter, for the next day Winchell ran a full column attack on Liebler.

One of Liebler's assistants reported: "Winchell has somebody checking on you. He's offering money for dirt about you."

"If he's going to be that way about it, I'm not going to write his lousy letter," Liebler told Bill Ryan.

And he didn't.

Later it was learned that it was Grace Appel who secured attorney J. Roland Sala for Pat Ward.

Joey Adams denied ever having met or known either girl.

But Winchell was no longer interested in Adams. Now he had to "get" Liebler.

The flood of innuendo and smear directed at Liebler included items like these:

One of the ass't d.a.'s (who threatens to "ruin" certain locals) is so vulnerable. His trips are not on public questions but on personal monkey business.

And:

Ass't d.a. Liebler apparently forgot that even Adam found out how dangerous it is foolin' around an Appel.

In reviewing a play, "Men of Distinction," Winchell wrote:

This farce about the Jelke set was a hurried flop. No wonder. The cast neglected to include the biggest farces in the case: Att'y J. Roland Sala and Ass't D.A. Liebler.

Commented Winchell on the Appel affair:

The fact is that for a woman to say she loves Walter Winchell is no attack on her credibility . . .

Winchell went gunning for Liebler's job. He suggested that an unnamed prosecutor was "unlawfully an ass't d.a." In his column he cajoled, pleaded with and threatened District Attorney Frank Hogan about Liebler.

When Hogan wouldn't bow to his suggestion, Winchell tried to hurt Hogan's rumored hopes for the mayorality nomination by writing:

Gov. Dewey has surrendered on swinging the mayorality nod to Dist. Att'y Hogan and is now romancing Judge David Peck . . .

When Winchell went gunning for a member of the Attorney-General's staff, Nathan Goldstein had hurried to ask for the man's resignation.

"My God, I don't want him angry with me," Goldstein is reported to have said. "I want to run for Governor of this State some day."

But District Attorney Frank J. Hogan was made of sterner stuff. Hogan had a spine.

He ignored the Winchell sniping.

Liebler had explained the reason for Winchell's fury to Hogan. Hogan never mentioned the matter again. It is not even certain that he saw the items intended to hurt him politically.

When Winchell received the "confidential report" on the private life of Anthony Liebler, he was sitting on his haunches in the presence of a press agent in the Stork Club.

It was a six page report. A newcomer to press agentry had paid almost $100 a page for it, in hopes of improving his stock with Winchell.

"How is it, Walter," asked the table acquaintance.

"Nuts," groaned Winchell. "This Dutch bastard doesn't do anything but go home at night. He's been married eighteen years and all he ever does is go home."

It was clearly a way of life Winchell couldn't fathom.

In his office, Liebler faced a reporter. "I don't see the column more than once or twice a week," Liebler said. He grinned. "That Winchell is supposed to be powerful. Newspapers and radio and television . . ."

"Have you ever made any attempt to straighten the whole thing out?"

Liebler shrugged. "Why bother." Then he became serious as he thought aloud. "I guess if I ever run for political office he'll do his worst."

"I guess so," said the reporter.

Liebler shrugged. "Well, we just ignore him. That's the only thing to do. Ignore him."

The phone rang and it was a midtown precinct who had just booked two prostitutes and wanted to know if Liebler recognized their names. He didn't.

He summoned two assistants.

They didn't know the girls either.

Nobody thought of wondering if Winchell knew the girls.

33

Decline

Walter Winchell was worried. Rigor mortis was setting in. From all parts of the country came reports that newspapers were dropping his column or cutting it down to a three inch box.

"I'm surprised at how little effect leaving him out altogether has on our readers," one editor reported. "We left the column out for many days without getting a single reader protest. We're thinking of dropping him when the current contract expires."

It was the same story in many towns and cities.

Editor Wallace Carroll of the Winston-Salem (N.C.) Twin-City Sentinel discarded the Winchell column after carrying it for more than ten years.

"We expected a few complaints when we dropped Winchell at the beginning of the year. But no convulsions occurred. In fact, we haven't had a letter or a phone call.

"Winchell was certainly good value in years past, but tastes change."

In the words "but tastes change" Carroll was writing Winchell's professional obituary. The product once greatly in demand was in demand no more.

The Charlotte (N.C.) Observer dropped the Winchell column in 1953. Again the report was that after two weeks there had not been a single phone call or letter asking about its absence.

By early 1953 the Winchell column began to shrink

and shrivel almost before it left New York City, and the Winchell television program was in even worse shape.

The two organizations that measure the size of audiences for the radio and television industry are Hooper and Nielsen.

One of the few things that competitors Hooper and Nielsen agreed about is that the size of Winchell's audiences were very small.

The facts upset Winchell so much that he complained to the trade magazine *Advertising Age* that Hooper and Nielsen were using the "wrong kind of arithmetic."

In February he wrote in his column that he was "up" in his Nielsen for "an increase of 30 per cent." What he meant was that the lowest rating he has ever had in his life went just a little bit higher than the lowest rating he has ever had in his life.

Winchell couldn't adjust to the fact that he seemed to be on the way out. He still talked about his "coast to coast" television show although his telecast was only going to nineteen stations. Eight others received a kinescope or film of the show and ran it late at night.

(One TV station manager inquired of the network if it would be okey to run the film the following day "among the afternoon soap operas.")

In 1953 the frenetic Winchell became nervous as a can of worms.

Television viewers who were puzzled by Winchell's practice of bouncing up and down in his chair were unaware that Winchell was suffering from what country folk refer to as "the outhouse trots."

Winchell's multiplying feuds, plus the poor showing he was making with radio, television and his column didn't help his chronic diarrhea, with which he had suffered for years. It kept him from sleeping a night through without interruptions.

Doctors were unable to treat it successfully and told him that it's psychosomatic.

Since the time more than a year before when he

pleaded with Joe McCarthy not to attack him, and a few weeks later gave tacit approval to anti-Negro discrimination in night clubs, Winchell became a pathetic figure: a lonely embittered man who wouldn't admit to himself that he no longer led the parade: that he had come to mean less and less to those whose respect he most needs —show business and newspaper people.

Winchell's declining importance was reflected in the people he associated with and the people and things he plugged.

For more than twenty years, prominent politicians, diplomats and writers had been his playmates. Now, most of them methodically avoided him.

He found himself plugging Joseph McCarthy, Frank Costello, and the girlie magazine *Confidential.*

Confidential's first issue had two anti-Negro articles and, since the Josephine Baker affair, Winchell relished that kind of perversion.

His favorite vacation place was Miami Beach, where Negroes are not permitted in the theatres, hotels or on the beach itself. He never uttered a word of protest.

In March when someone remarked that it was a shame Lena Horne couldn't live in a decent hotel when she was performing in a Miami Beach nightclub, the columnist shrugged his shoulders and asked, "Why do you want them living on the beach?"

Not far from the hotel Winchell winters at, is the Kennilworth Hotel, where Winchell's friend Arthur Godfrey usually stays when in Florida. Winchell wasn't allowed to live there because it was "restricted." No Jews allowed.

Confidential Magazine appealed to Winchell. He began his romance with the magazine by publishing this item:

Joe Louis threatens a suit (for $100,000) against the zingy new mag. Confidential . . .

(It wasn't true, of course. Louis had never heard of the magazine.)

To please Winchell, the magazine published a Winchell-fed smear on Barry Gray.

So, on February 16, Winchell's column carried these "payoff" items:

Confidential is preparing an article on a disc-jurq which will sell out the first day.

That mag is threatened with a suit (by a song star) for its current piece which calls him "fruity as a nut cake!"

The "suit" was the same tired makebelieve angle Winchell had used to plug *Confidential* with regards to Joe Louis.

The only article in the magazine about a song star was one on Johnny Ray. Nowhere in the article was Ray called "fruity as a nut cake."

How did the "national" plug for *Confidential* Magazine fare?

Out of New York, Winchell's two most important papers were the *Miami Herald* and the *Washington Post*.

Both the *Herald* and the *Post* omitted the item.

In the *Herald,* the Winchell column appeared three days late. ("Nobody is in any hurry to read him," a *Herald* editor told a visiting author. "He isn't liked in this town. He knows enough to keep away from the *Herald* office when he's in Miami," the editor said.)

The *Herald* cut five inches out of the column.

The *Washington Post* cut Winchell's 26 inch column to 12 inches. This was about par for the course.

Of four other papers that "buy" Winchell, two hadn't bothered to carry the column. One carried only four inches, or less than one-eighth of the original column. One carried ten inches, or less than one-half.

(Winchell was aware that his courtesy plugs for people and products didn't usually appear in most out-of-town papers. The press agents knew it too. Fortunately for them, most clients didn't know it. When they saw their name in the *New York Mirror* they believed people all over the country would see it.)

When the National Association for the Advancement

of Colored People was about to take Josephine Baker's side in the Stork Club Jim Crow incident, a press agent told NAACP public relations man Henry Moon that the NAACP would be foolish.

"Winchell's good will is important," the press agent declared "His plugs . . ."

"What about his plugs?" Moon wanted to know. "He plugged a book I wrote. Do you know how many copies we sold because of that plug? Two."

The press agent reported the incident to Winchell, who was only a few weeks away from the nervous breakdown that he was to suffer.

Winchell telephoned to NAACP director Walter White.

"You have someone named Moon working for you. Do you know what he had the nerve to say?"

At this point, Winchell broke down and wept. White was on the phone trying to calm him for almost half an hour.

(More recently Winchell was talking to Arthur Godfrey about the Damon Runyon fund.

("They'll remember Runyon," he said. Tears came to his eyes. "No one will ever do this for me.")

Despite all the evidence, Winchell was scheming to regain his prestige. He liked to latch onto sure things and plug them—later taking bows for making them hits.

Hearing that the Bette Davis show "Two's Company" was sold out for three months in advance of its opening, he began to praise it daily as soon as the New York critics gave it poor reviews.

Then he wrote that he was "filling the theatre."

"Who needs critics," he wrote. "Just get Winchell to plug it."

In a single column he carried both of these plugs:

They were discussing "Two's Company" and the 151 backers who were saved by star Bette Davis . . . Several backers were overheard panning it between acts at the premiere . . . This hit again convinced us that Backers are a dime-a-dz. on Broadway, but Backbone is still rare . . . There is no coincidence in the two Ts in the star's first name. They stand for Terrific Trouper. There are two Ts in Bette and two in Talent.

And:

From ticket broker G. Solotaire: "Just a fast line to tell you it must have been your review on 'Two's Company,' since you were alone in appraising it as a click. The Bette Davis show was the biggest and toughest ticket to get for the 3rd night. You couldn't even buy a 'single' at 3 p.m., a dozen hours after the Mirror's notice hit the stands." (The show had standees the 2nd night, and the advance sale took a hefty jump.)

But a short time later when the advance sale had run its course, the box office revenue slumped badly and the show's producer closed the show.

After that Winchell carried the false story that Bette Davis had cancer.

And when that was denied, he carried the vindictive false story that "The Bette Davis show lost a total investment of $300,000."

He followed this up in a few days with:

Bette Davis is threatened with a lawsuit by the "Two's Company" owners. Over the $300,000 foldo. Her operation (it is feared) will leave her lips numb for six months.

"That son of a bitch!" Bette Davis said on reading it, her lips perfectly mobile.

34

—And Fall

The scarecrow had begun to come apart. First a sleeve, then the shirt, then the straw filling.

On May 3, 1953, Winchell frankly admitted that he had come to the end "of another very tired broadcast."

He was making a valiant if unsuccessful attempt to recapture a part of the gigantic audience that once was his. He featured two contests on his program simultaneously: one giving away dogs, another horses.

Each television show would feature four or five film or night club stars. In return for their appearance, he would plug their current activity.

But he was no longer the unapproachable Winchell. Before Betty Grable or Marilyn Monroe would consent to appear, their studio press agents insisted on knowing exactly what kind of plug he would deliver.

Nothing helped.

Despite his almost daily double talk ("The Neilsen teevy and radio WW ratings are up 2 points each," he wrote on June 1, "and we have only 15 minutes to get a rating. The opposition has half an hour!") his listener rating continued to fall.

"The advance Neilsen (television) index for the two weeks just ended gives the W.W. Sunday nighter a jump of 2 points," he wrote.

The Neilsen people said they didn't know what he was talking about.

Week after week the ratings came out. Where once he

had been top man, Winchell was now no longer among the top twenty.

The American Broadcasting Company issued a press release on April 10, beginning "WALTER WINCHELL, radio's highest rated newsman according to a majority of the accredited surveys . . ."

But under questioning, the network was unable to name any current "accredited" survey which he topped. One ABC publicity man jested, "Maybe we meant the average of all of them over the years . . ."

Meanwhile, Winchell dug deeper into his feuds. He was now so involved in personal vendettas that *Time* magazine reported "editors were cutting or killing many of his columns" because "editors and readers outside of Manhattan often didn't know what Winchell was talking about."

Where it was once fashionable to carry Winchell, it was now fashionable not to carry him.

Dwight Pennington, feature editor of the *Kansas City Star* said proudly: "The *Star* has never carried the Walter Winchell column. It was used in the *Kansas City Journal-Post*, and apparently didn't do them much good, for that paper quit publication in 1941."

There were two "important" papers in the Winchell orbit. One was the *New York Mirror* and the other, the *Washington Post*. The *Mirror*, his home paper, was a shoddy imitation of the *New York Daily News*. It was the *Mirror* which copyrighted the column and then turned it over to the Hearst syndicate.

The *Washington Post* published the column simultaneously with the *Mirror*. Other papers carried the column one or two days later.

The *Washington Post* was a dignified newspaper, and it became more and more discontented with the daily Winchell.

Managing Editor James R. Wiggins junked at least one

out of three columns. "Mostly because of its content," he explained. "Sometimes because we don't have time to check for libel."

When the Winchell column did appear in the *Washington Post* in 1953, it was usually found in the last pages of the paper, among the comic strips.

After polling its member papers, the Western Newspaper Union decided to drop the Winchell column. Within one year, more than 500 dailies and weeklies had discontinued Winchell.

On July 24, 1953 he was appearing in 178 papers, and three had given notice of termination of contract.

He tried to give the impression it wasn't so.

On May 13 he reported, "The colyums newest boss (among the Syndicut) is the Houston (Texas) Chronicle, one of the Nation's leading papyri . . ."

But even as his column began in that paper, a *Chronicle* columnist, Charlie Evans, chatted about the *Chronicle's* story on water pressure in Houston. The story had been written by staffer Mel Young and had been picked up nationally.

It seems that the water pressure indicated when people were leaving their t.v. sets for the bathroom. There were pronounced drops in pressure during the commercials.

Evans reported: "The chart shows water pressure highest during the Robert Montgomery show. Lowest pressure, indicating most folks are away from their sets, is recorded during the Walter Winchell program."

A city desk man at the *Chronicle* said: "There is a vast disinterest in Winchell in the newsroom here. Most of us find him dull as dishwater. But, oh, for another Odd McIntyre."

"There appears to have been some pressure from somewhere to level the Winchell fulminations into our paper. As much as hinted by one of the execs who must listen to the constant advice from the business office."

Following Winchell's admission that he had been a red dupe, the column was conspicuously absent from the pages of the *Houston Chronicle*.

"Winchell columns are being withheld to determine what the public reaction is," explained the feature editor.

Harry Golden, a publisher, wrote in his *Carolina Israelite* in February:

"The local newspaper has not printed a Winchell column in quite some time now. Five or six years ago I would have probably called the managing editor and asked about it. I am sure that quite a few others would have done the same. But I have no inclination to do so now. I doubt seriously whether the publisher has received a single phone call since he decided to omit the Winchell column. Mr. Winchell in recent years has tried a new twist on 'how to influence people.' He has antagonized his friends and well-wishers, while those people whom he has tried to please have always hated him, and I am sure he hasn't succeeded in endearing himself to them yet.

"His broadcast a day or two before the election last November was so violent an attack on Mr. Truman that it probably made even Senator McCarthy blush. Mr. Winchell pulled out all the stops and called Mr. Truman a 'Ku Kluxer.' Can you imagine that? There was no one left in America for Mr. Winchell to call a 'Ku Kluxer' except Mr. Truman. It must have embarrassed Mr. Truman's most outspoken enemies. President Truman established the State of Israel, (without Truman we would have had to wait another one hundred years); he proposed full Embassy status for the Catholic Vatican; and he was pilloried in the South for his 'civil rights' program for the Negroes. Some Ku Kluxer! A few more 'Ku Kluxers' like Mr. Truman and I am afraid we would soon experience what Isaiah called the 'Brotherhood of Man.'"

And in June, Golden wrote:

"For years I have associated the charming voice of Milton Cross with the parting of the hold curtain at the Metropolitan Opera House in New York. Everytime I heard the cultured tones of Milton Cross I immediately thought of Mimi dying of tuberculosis in 'La Boheme,' or of the Prize Song in the 'Meistersinger.' Think of my surprise when I happened to tune in on Walter Winchell the other night, for the first time in a year or more, and heard that fine Milton Cross accent introduce the wild hysteria of Walter Winchell! Why, sacrilege, is what I call it! It's like asking Professor Albert Einstein to introduce Father Divine."

The critics were shooting thick and fast.

Winchell's radio and television sponsor reported "only one out of three letters that come to us is unfavorable."

But the commentator's remarks about Presidential candidate Stevenson, his tacit approval of Jim Crow, and other strange manifestations of the weakened Winchell had caused many people (including jewelers) to inform the sponsor (the Gruen Watch Company) that Gruen would be boycotted on a permanent basis.

By mid-1953, Gruen had decided to sponsor only "every other Winchell broadcast and television show."

Two months after it was announced that alternate weeks were open and would be available, no second sponsor had come forward with a bid, and as summer approached, the network began to make frantic "special offers" to entice a sponsor.

There had been a time when sponsors waited in line: when Winchell could have had his pick of a dozen of the biggest.

"The size of the audience doesn't mean anything," he said. "What really counts is do you sell the product!" And: "I am happy to report an extra dividend of 20¢ and the regular quarterly dividend of 20¢ a share were declared on the Common Stock of the Gruen Watch Company for payment July 1st. No extra was paid last year."

Winchell repeated this with variations every day or two for a month.

Still no new sponsor appeared.

Potential sponsors may have read the Gruen annual statement. Watch sales were below expectations. The profit increase and extra dividend could be attributed to "profitable defense work."

At last, at the end of July, the makers of Carter's Little Liver pills agreed to take on the alternate weeks at a special rate. They would use the time to sell a shaving cream that spouted from the can.

Because the Carter people knew they were in the driver's seat, they decided not to begin sponsorship until mid-October, when the listening rating was likely to be highest.

Gruen then agreed to sponsor the three empty weeks at discounts and with tieup promotions given as an inducement by the ABC network.

It was enough to make even Winchell blanch.

He'd once sat in the top radio and column spot. He'd been hymned and greased by actors, politicians, writers, diplomats. He'd been revered by millions and was considered "the most powerful" newspaperman in the land.

Now, as he fell swiftly, his column could hardly be distinguished from the columns of a hundred imitators. And the barking and yelping on radio and television could hardly be distinguished from what might come from the throat of a snootzer-poodle.

On September 6, 1953 he returned, this time on a simultaneous broadcast and television show.

His face was haggard. New thicker lenses had been placed in his eyeglasses. These he held in his hand and shook at the television audience as he lectured to it.

Only his irresponsibility was the mixture as before.

He announced excitedly, "The number one female star of television is a member of the Communist Party. In a secret hearing of a Congressional Committee she was shown her Communist Party card."

So that it could be lost on no one, he repeated it solemnly. This was the number one "scoop" of the night. This was Winchell, the "inside" man at work again.

Business as usual.

Most of his audience knew, of course, that the "number one female star of television" could be none other than Lucille Ball. Her "I Love Lucy" show led all the rest in popularity ratings.

It was a matter of hours before Lucille Ball could counter with the information that in 1936 she had registered to vote for the Communist ticket as a favor to her grandfather. She had voted the Communist ticket that year. Seventeen years ago.

The next year she had registered as a Democrat. Eventually she became a registered Republican.

She never was and is not now a member of the Communist Party.

The Congressional Committee who had questioned her promptly announced that she was being honest in her statement and that there was no reason for the Committee to believe that Miss Ball had been mixed up with the Communists at any time or in any way.

The "scoop" about a Communist party card was a pure Winchellism: a total and deliberate lie.

One week later, Winchell hadn't bothered to retract or apologize. He was too busy trying to wreck other careers, twisting his warped facts so they might draw other blood, so that they might ruin other reputations, other lives.

35

Requiem

Walter Winchell was tired.

He'd once written that most benefits were "unwillingly given and are chiefly for advertising." But in the Spring of 1953 he thought he would prove that he hadn't toppled. He announced that he was sponsoring a benefit for the widows of New York police and firemen killed in the line of duty.

Two weeks before the Monday night benefit, an S.O.S. went out to all Hearst columnists and all cooperative disk jockeys to plug the benefit. Tickets weren't selling.

It was the biggest advertising and promotion campaign New York had seen in years. It was for a worthy cause.

Only one seat in four was filled in Madison Square Garden on the night of March 16.

His attempt to resurrect himself had failed.

To avoid a process server in a libel suit, he flew to Hollywood. Jane Kean was there. There too, 20th-Century-Fox treated him royally, offered him his fill of chauffered Cadillacs, women and private screenings.

The Hearst organization decided to throw a "testimonial" to him in Los Angeles.

More than four hundred California newspapermen were invited. About eighty attended.

High spot of the evening was Winchell's emotional

speech. He started to say thank you, and continued to talk for ninety minutes.

"They accuse me of keyhole peeping," he said. "They've had Yale locks for the past 30 years."

He said that editors who laughed at his Stork Club statesmanship were lacking in news sense "because my Washington stuff comes straight from the top men in government."

He ranted against the "ingrates" who had "turned" on him. He was especially bitter about Drew Pearson.

He blamed the numerous attacks on him as "the influence of Commies and Commie stooges in some editorial rooms."

For an hour and a half he poured out his heartache and his hatreds, and then he sighed and sat down suddenly, staring at a room full of embarrassment.

That week, too, at a party at the Friar's Club, George Jessel delivered a lyrical introduction for Winchell.

The columnist seized another chance to blast his "enemies" and leveled most of this attack on Ed Sullivan, who was somehow managing to best him as the final curtain neared.

A few days later the Sullivan column revealed that it was Jessel who had bored his table companions a few weeks before at an ASCAP dinner in New York by talking incessantly about "what a complete no-good" Winchell was.

He returned to New York.

He received "the 1953 Mike and Screen Press Award of the Radio-Newsreel-Television Working Press Association of New York," a publicity promotion.

He received the award in a near-empty room. The dinner, a promotion, was a financial flop, with the empty seats outnumbering those that were filled.

The only "working press association" that counted

among newspapermen was the American Newspaper Guild. Winchell had left that years before, when he turned against all unions.

The commission on Freedom of the Press had criticized the pitchmen of the press who had injected artificial sensation and manufactured suspense into their operation.

"The worst offenders in this direction are to be found among the newspaper columnists and radio commentators," the Commission declared. "The members of this craft have come to perform an indispensable function in American public discussion. But they must attract the maximum audience, too. Some of them have thought that the way to do this is to supply the public with keyhole gossip, rumor, character assassination, and lies."

Winchell didn't reply.

He kept more to himself.

Like Walter, June Winchell was lonely.

But she had always been lonely while his life was full. To occupy her time she'd once adopted two Chinese children. Winchell made her give them up. Shortly afterward she had a nervous breakdown.

When he came home a few weeks later to find a little Negro boy whom she planned to adopt, he threatened never to come home again unless "you get that brat out of here."

In 1951, she underwent serious surgery in New York.

Winchell reported to his radio audience that she was "doing fine"—from Florida.

More recently she suffered a heart attack. Now she rests in Phoenix, Arizona, filling some of her hours with a visiting psychiatrist.

Once in a while he tries to recapture the past.

He leaves his top-floor suite at the St. Moritz hotel at about seven in the evening.

He still pays about $400 a month for a suite that would cost anyone else $1200 a month. Once, when the management hinted that they felt entitled to a raise, Winchell attacked the St. Moritz in his column for three days in a row.

The management has never mentioned the subject of a rent raise again.

(Something else unchanged at the St. Moritz is the size of the tips he gives bellboys. They're still ten cents.)

He wanders along Sixth Avenue, unrecognized.

On Fifty-Third Street he turns east for the Stork Club.

Sometimes, in the early morning hours after the club has closed, he cruises around in his car equipped with its police radio. His companion is usually a Hearst employee, who doesn't mind being associated with Winchell—for whatever publicity it will bring him.

The companion, radio columnist Jack O'Brian, years before had wanted to start a 'Hate Winchell Club.'

Early in the morning, when Broadway is pulling a blanket over her head, he drops into a soda fountain for an ice cream soda.

Then home, to his lonely rooms that overlook Manhattan.

His staccato radio delivery has slowed up.

He has slowed up.

At five or six in the morning he edits a column submitted by a ghostwriter or assembles and edits the scores of terse items submitted by the press agents.

"Don't run two columns alike," Hellinger had once told him. "Keep your readers off balance. Keep 'em guessing."

He'd keep 'em guessing. He'd show 'em.

That awful feeling is with him again. "They" are trying to get rid of him. The feeling that has haunted him all his life.

In a little while, daylight will come over Central Park.

Texas Guinan is dead. Sime Silverman is dead. Jimmy Walker is dead. Mark Hellinger is dead. Damon Runyon is dead.

He sits, far above the early morning noises of the city, alone and bitter, a man who has outlived the era of his own greatness.

Soon his long night will be over. The first light will unwrap the darkness that blankets Central Park. The haze will lift as the early sunlight heralds the big wonderful new tomorrow.

And soon he will sleep.

The two men sat in the Newspaper Room of the New York Public Library on West 25th Street.

Joseph Whalen, who had been doing research for this book, turned to his companion. "Do you know, I've read thousands of these columns and outside of what I've written down, I can't remember a damned thing from one of them."

"I know."

Whalen shook his head. "There isn't anything quite so stale as yesterday's Winchell gossip column."

The two men sat in moody silence. Winchell had made the written word sing for money, and the money would live after the song.

"He failed," Whalen said. "Do you realize that? All his life he's been a failure. The biggest failure of our time in the newspaper business."

"I know," the other man said.

Lost in thought, Whalen ran his hand across a Winchell column in the bound volume that was open before him.

The paper had yellowed. And now, at his touch, it began to crack into small pieces.